Gnomes

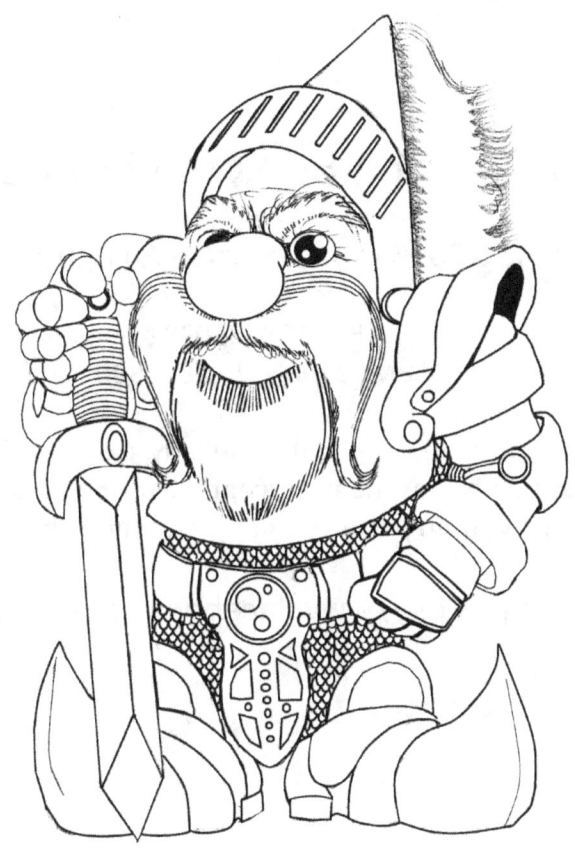

An Adult Coloring Book of Gnomes Throughout Time

By Daniel Savage

Gnomes: An Adult Coloring Book of Gnomes Throughout Time

ISBN: 1539850331
ISBN-13: 987-1539850335

Daniel Savage| https://www.facebook.com/savagescribbles/

Acknowledgements

My name is Daniel Savage and this coloring book is a collection of my work over the past two years (give or take a month or so). Creating these drawings for you was a true labor of love. I have always enjoyed art and feared it at the same time. I experience the most intense anxiety from the thought of showing someone what I have drawn, I tremble with fear whenever I show my work to anyone and yet here I am – preparing to sell a book! To say that I am terrified would be understating the irrational emotions that I feel. I have always doubted my artistic abilities and questioned whether anyone would enjoy the art that I have to offer. It took my 10-year-old daughter, Katie, a fellow artist to convince me to give this a shot. With a loving smile and an encouraging hug, she told me that I had something to offer the world – I just had to try. "Do your best daddy" became all I needed to hear. Thank you, my sweet Katie Bug – daddy did his best.

My family has struggled over the past recent years and when I decided to create this coloring book I was a man on a mission. I decided that I was going to dive into the world of self-publishing and at the very least, try to lift my family out of the extreme poverty that we found ourselves in. As I began creating the drawings for this coloring book, I increasingly felt sick. At first, I thought that I was working too many hours between my full-time job and my ambitious goals with this book. Not feeling well became the new norm for me and I tried to push past it and ignore how I was feeling. I was becoming depressed and angry with myself for being too tired to draw and would force myself to put some time in, every single day, even when I felt like I was going to fall out of my chair from exhaustion.

As it turns out, I am sick. After seeing a doctor for a few months, I ended up in the local emergency room where I found out that I have been suffering with stage IV metastatic cancer and I am terminal. This coloring book was to be the first step to becoming a better husband and father. It was to be the beginning of providing a better life for my family – a better future. It was my chance to not have to worry about the bills or if we had a nutritious meal on the table. My first step has turned into my last – this coloring book is my legacy instead of my beginning.

I want to personally thank you for purchasing this coloring book. Because of you, my children are able to sleep in a warm bed and eat a healthy meal. I feel at peace knowing that I will have left a little piece of myself in this world that can possibly continue to help my family once I am gone and can no longer be there for them. It has been a difficult journey, but it has been a beautiful one. Thank you for helping me help my family.

If you haven't heard of The Bloggess or Jennifer Lawson, author of, *Let's Pretend This Never Happened* and *Furiously Happy* run – do not walk, run out and grab a copy of her books. Find her blog online and get to know Jennifer Lawson, she is an amazing writer; an amazing person. I have followed The Bloggess since my wife introduced me to her in 2015 - right before I decided to create this coloring book. Something about her resonated with us and we read her books together. We have both struggled with depression and Jenny's books helped us to realize that a little crazy is the new normal and we could do this. Thank you for inspiring us Jenny and for being our unknowing cheerleader via your blog.

Through the love that grew from the bloggess, a Facebook group, "Saint James Garfield or simply SJG", was formed. This group is made up of a group of people who are truly saints. They have formed beautiful friendships that span the globe and spread love and help to those in need. I want to thank this group for not only helping my family, but for all that they have done for everyone that has come in contact with them. The saints of SJG are truly a wonderful group of people and deserve recognition for their selfless acts. A very special thank you to Jen, April, Noeline, Zoe, Beth, Stephanie, Kim, Shannon, Dawn, and Erin.

As I dove into researching how I was going to accomplish my goal of publishing my very first adult coloring book, I stumbled upon a YouTube video that directed me to yet another amazing Facebook group named, CBAS or Coloring Book Author Support. Without the amazing artists from this group, this coloring book would not be finished. To all of you – I cannot thank you enough for everything that you have done for my family. You are an amazing group of people and I am honored to have met you.

Lastly, I want to thank my wife, Mary, and my two beautiful children, Cody and Katie. Thank you for being there every step of the way and for believing in me. Thank you for cheering me on when I felt my work wasn't good enough, for excitedly discussing this project every single day, and for helping me come up with fun ideas for the drawings in this book. Thank you for being the best family I could have hoped for. I love you with every ounce of who I am.

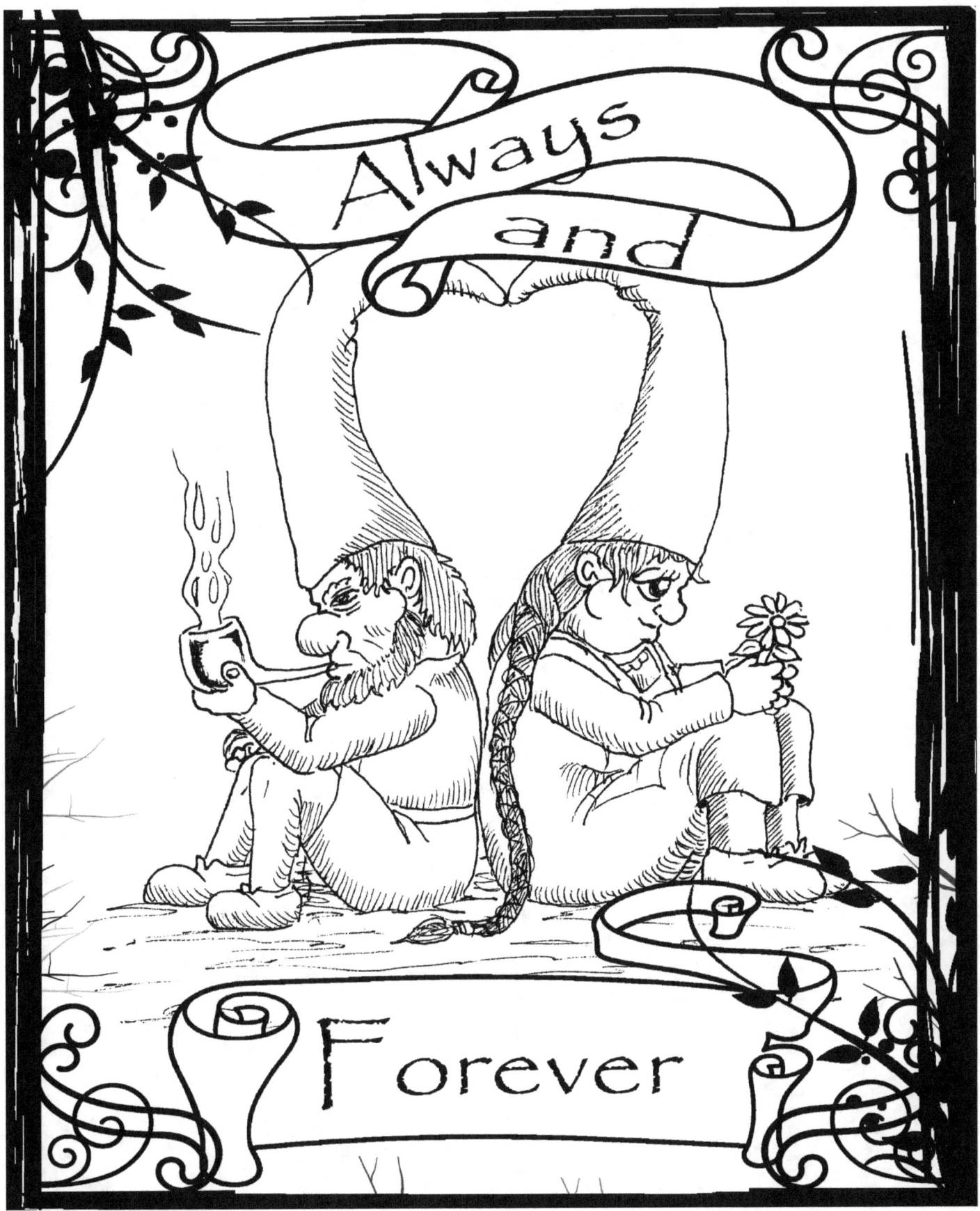

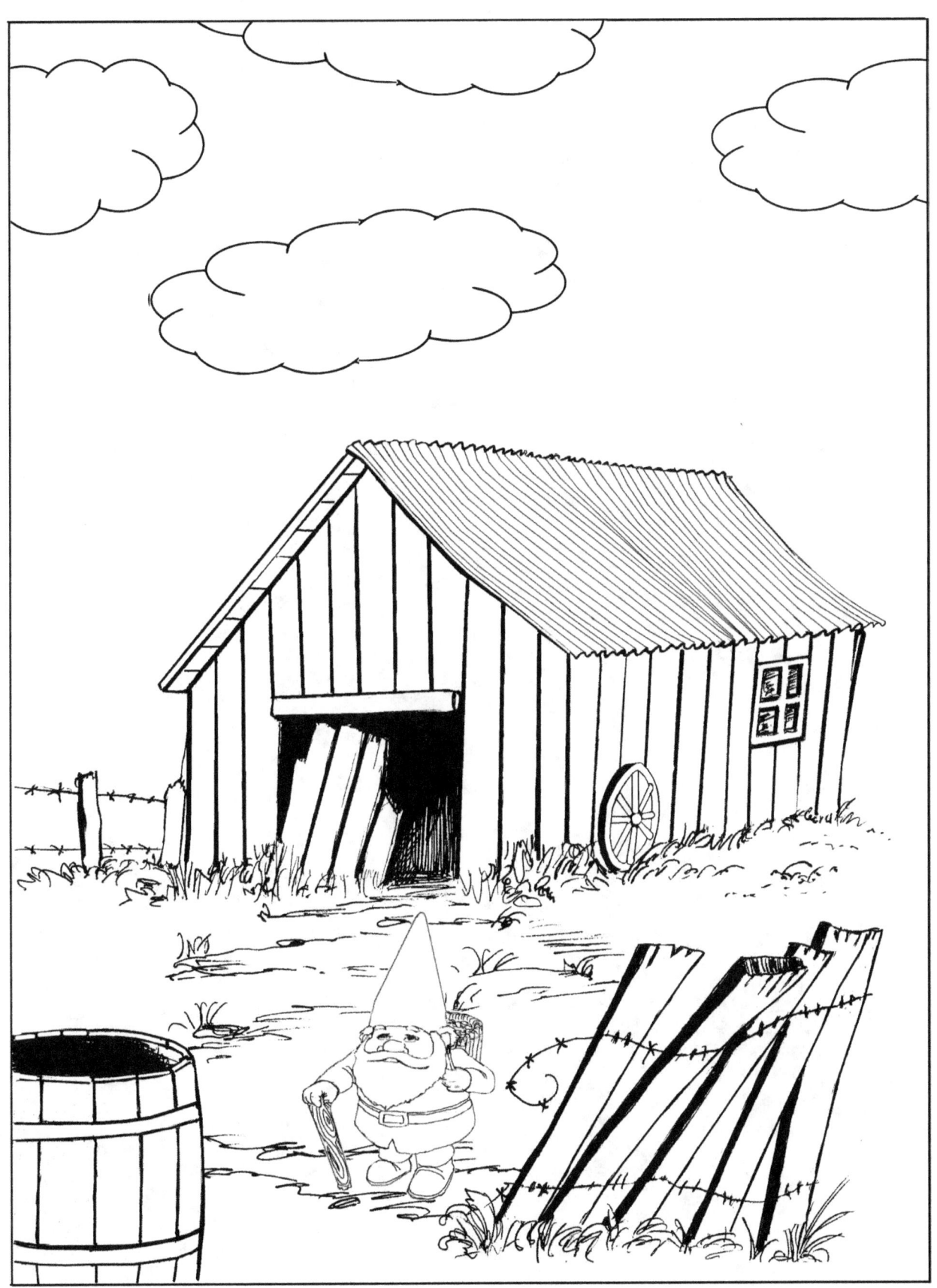

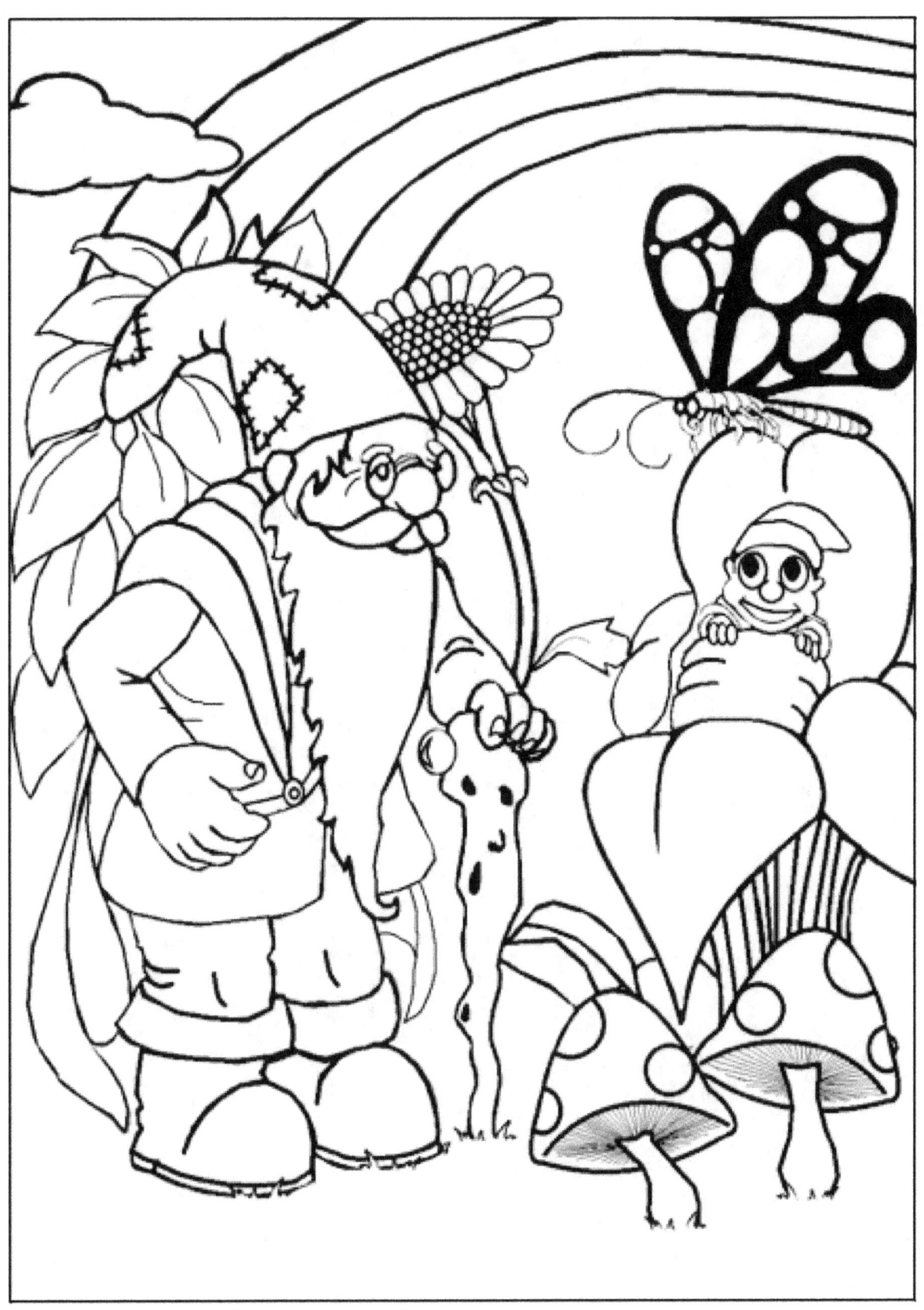

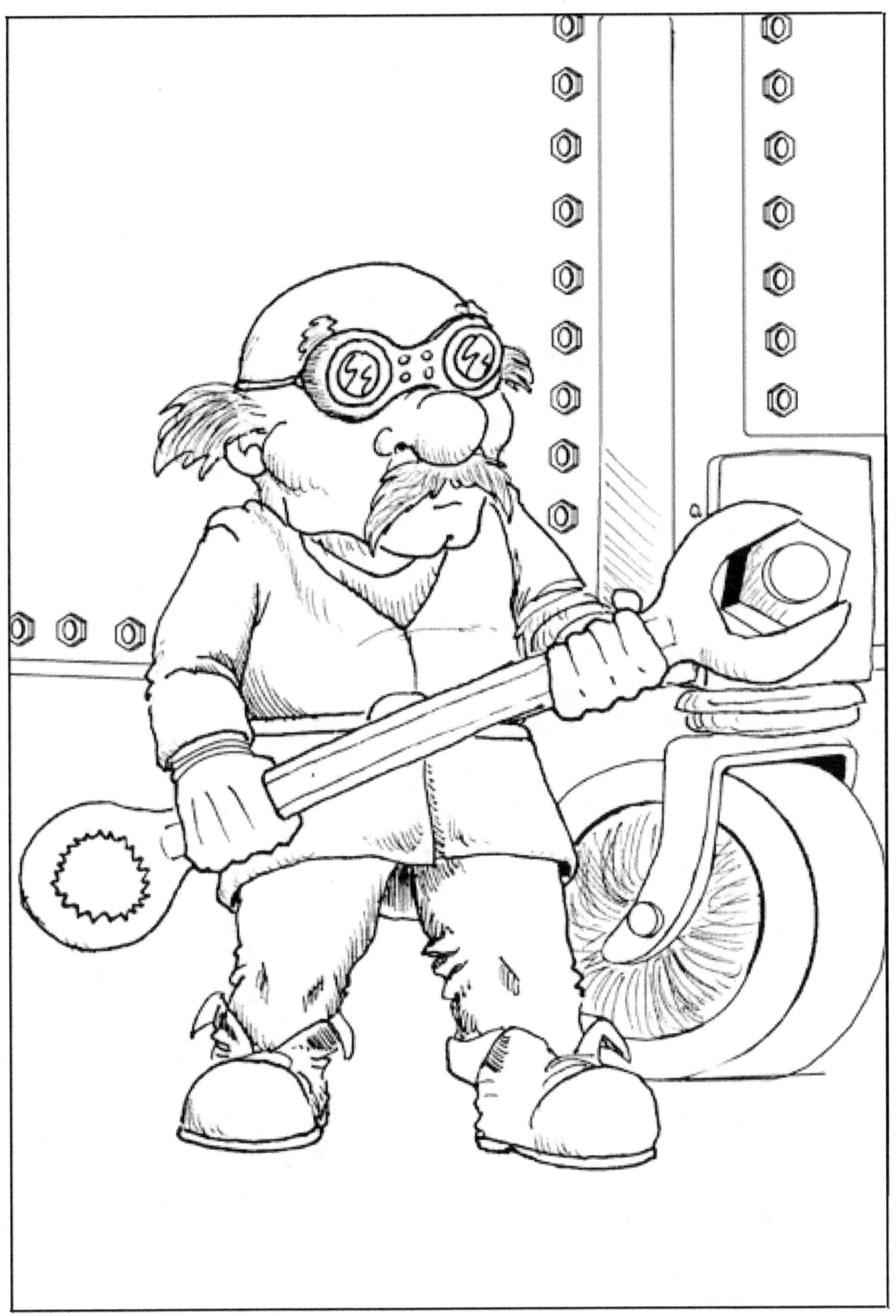

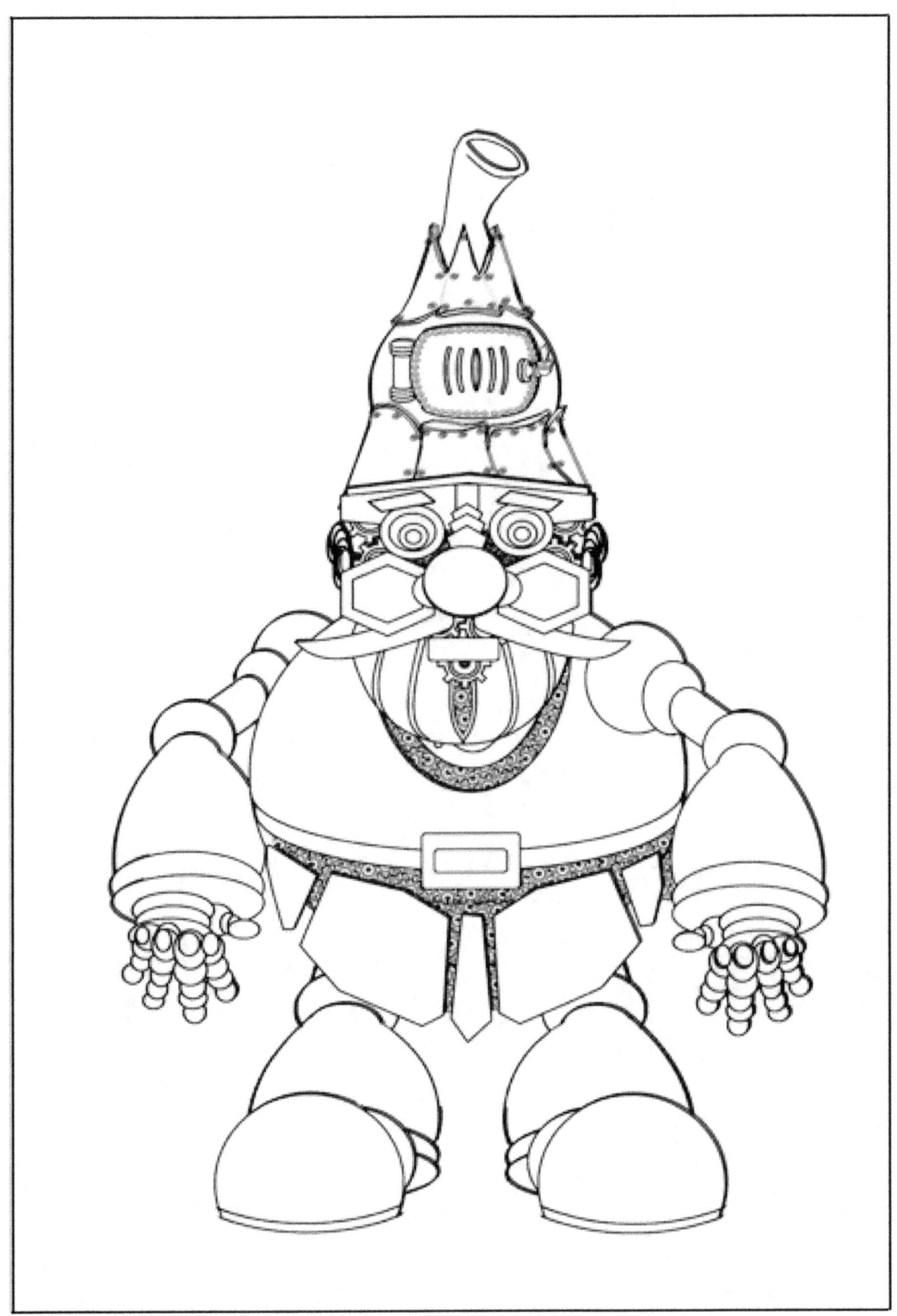

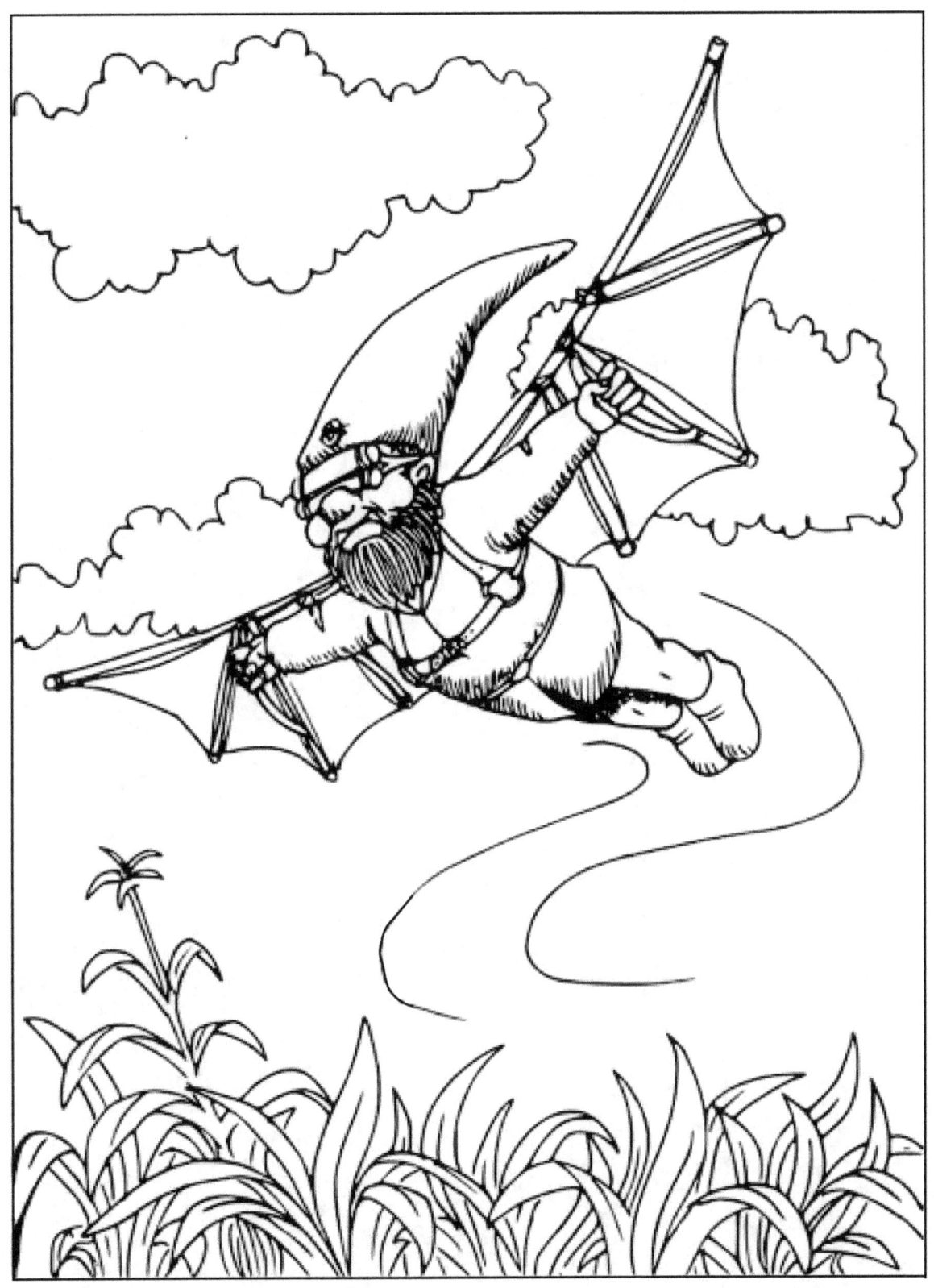

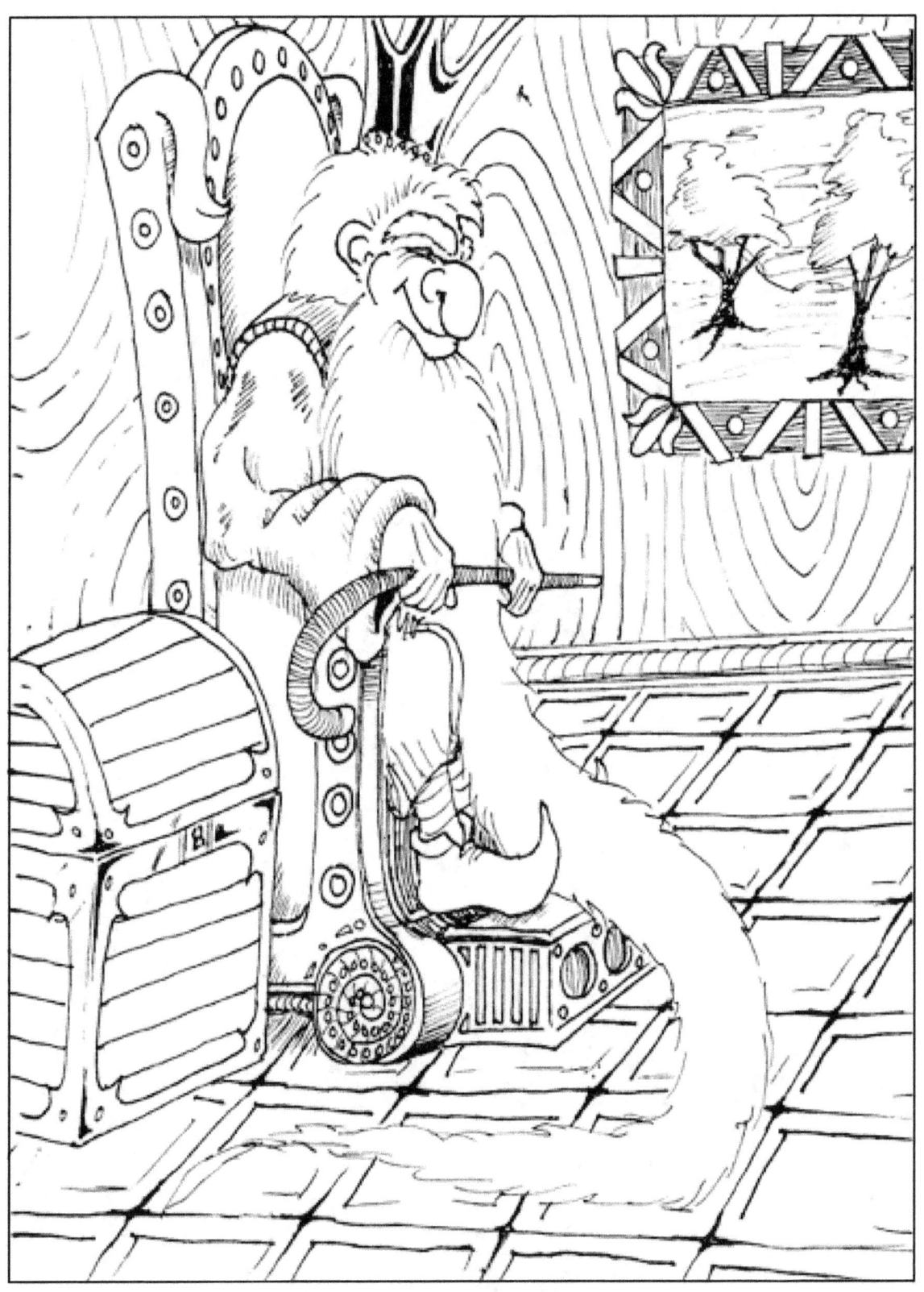

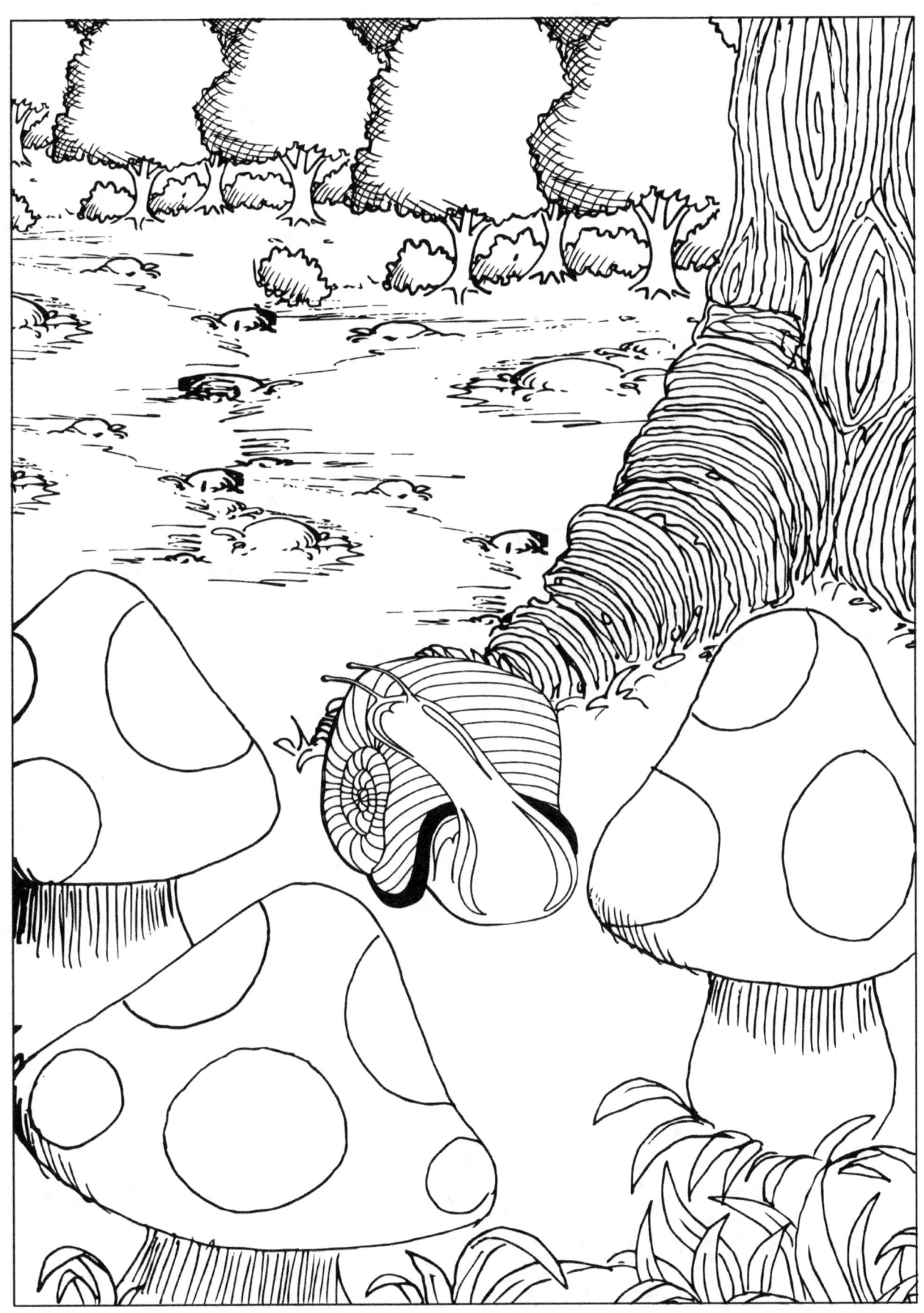

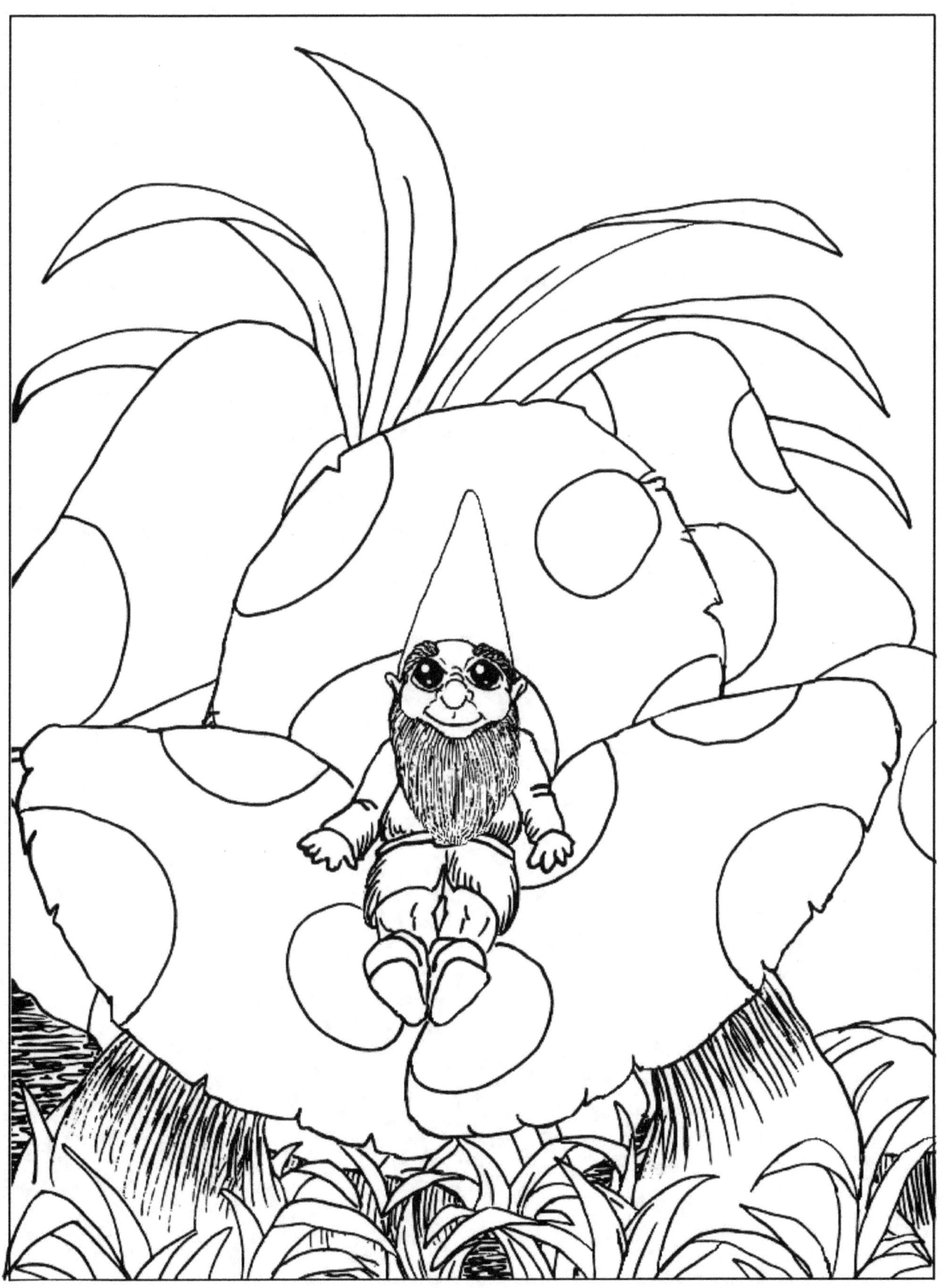

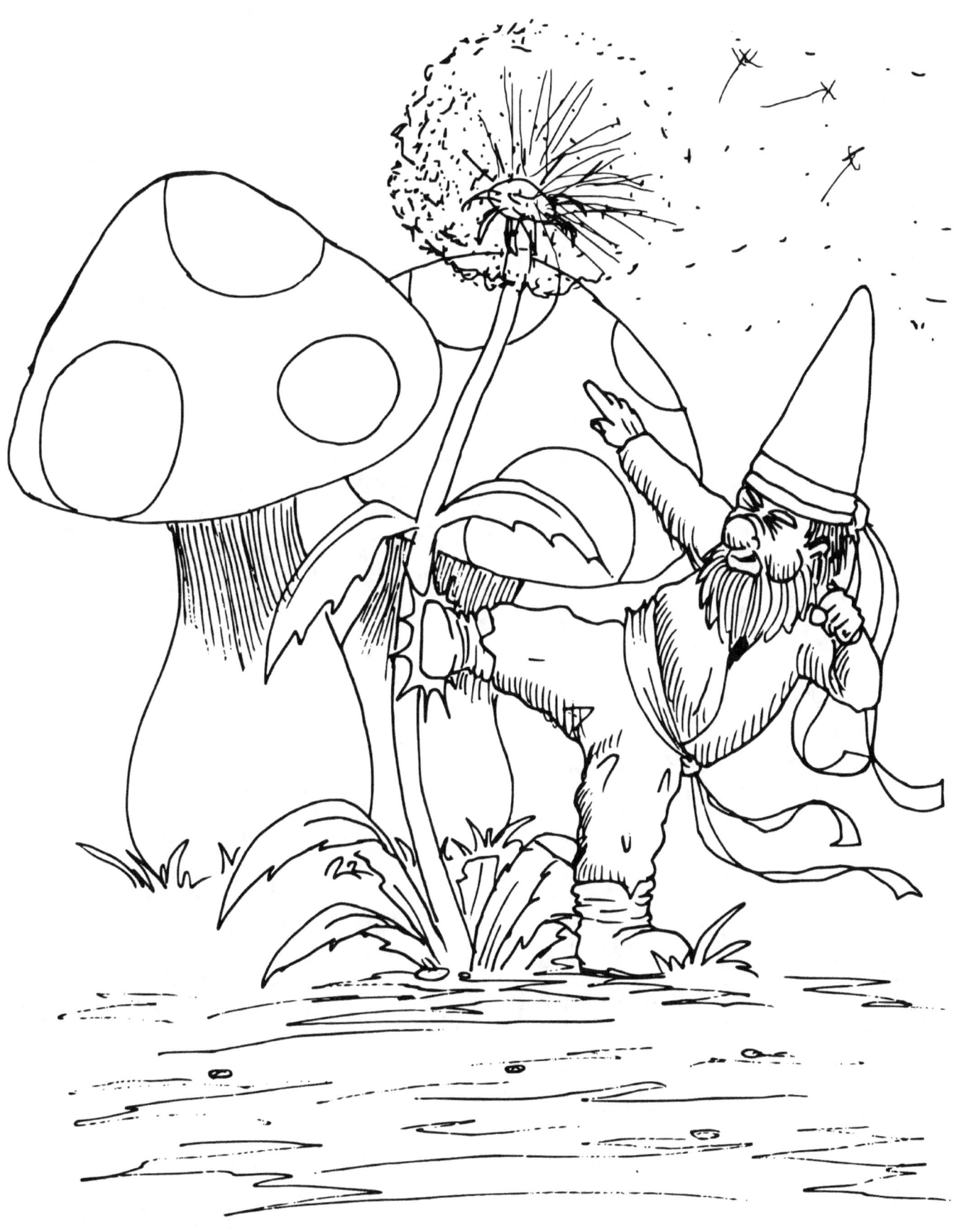

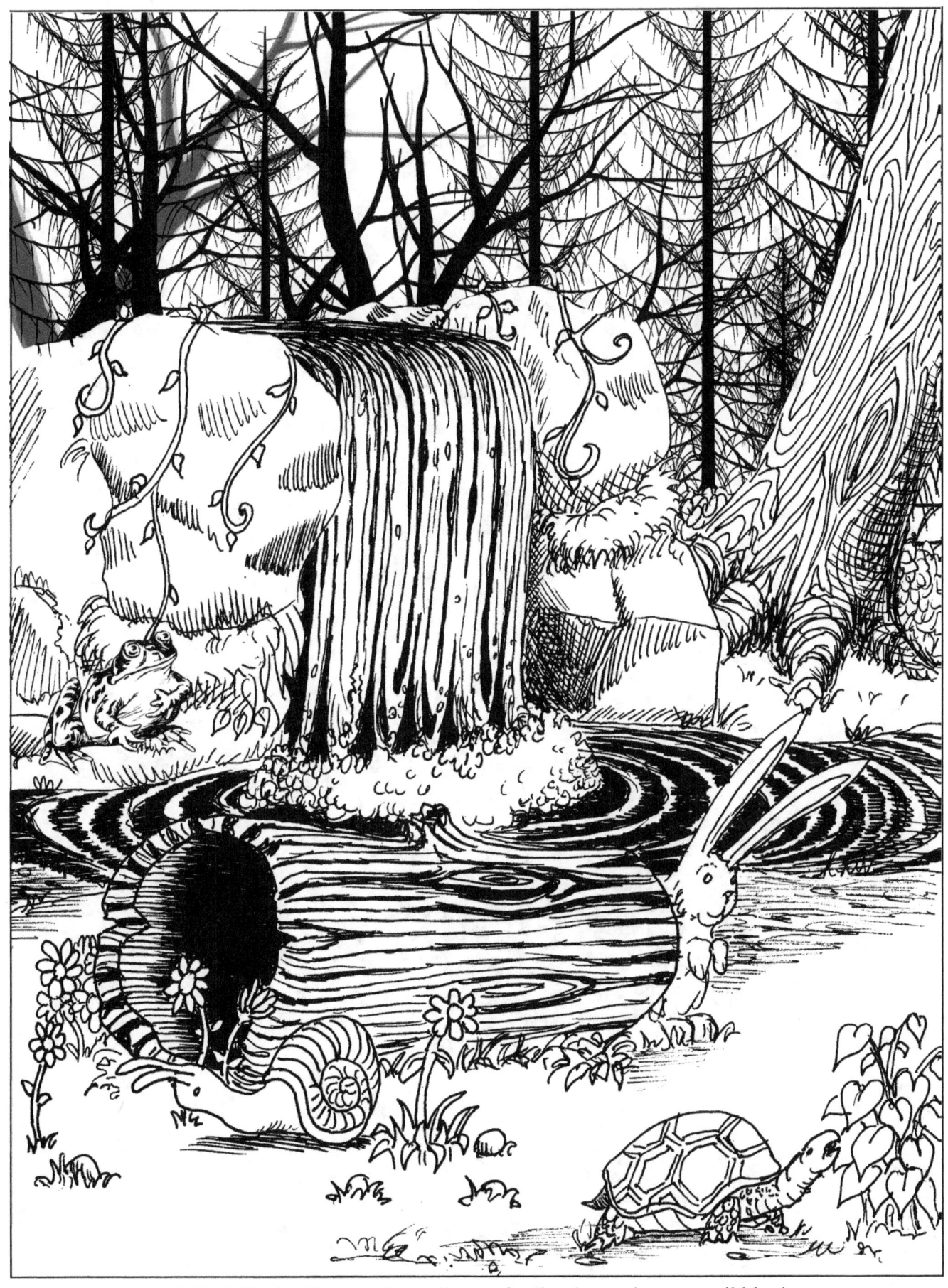

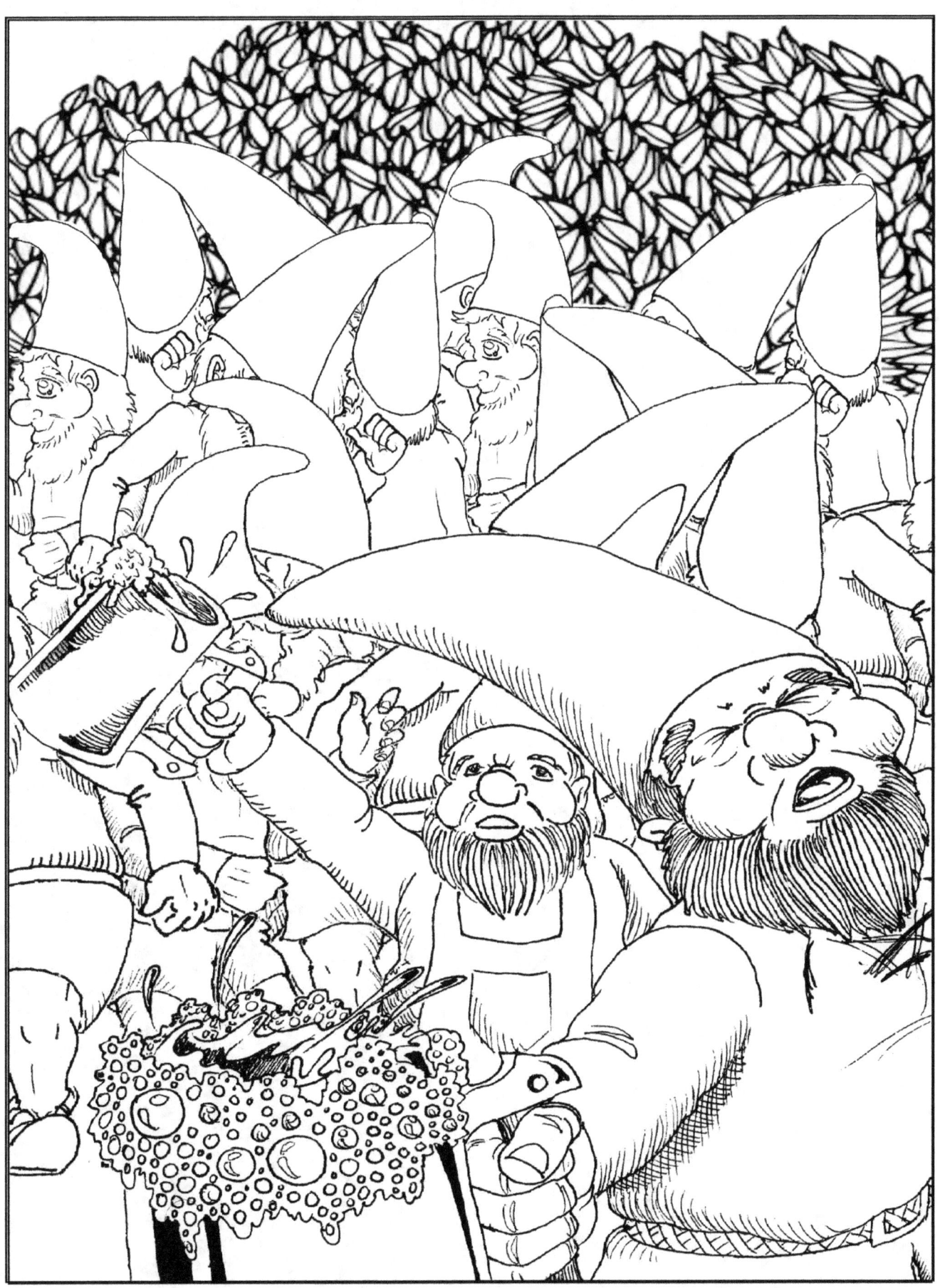

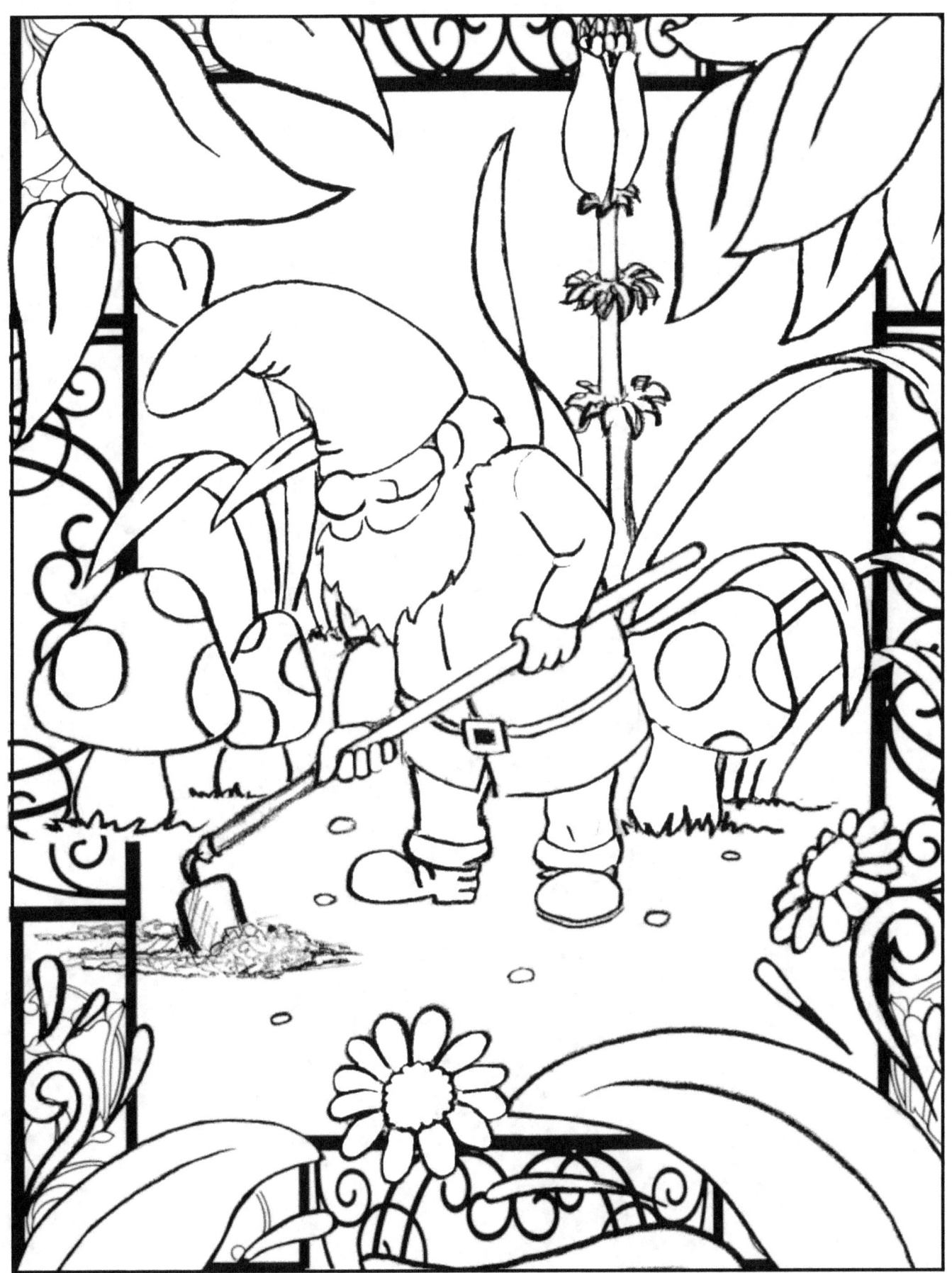

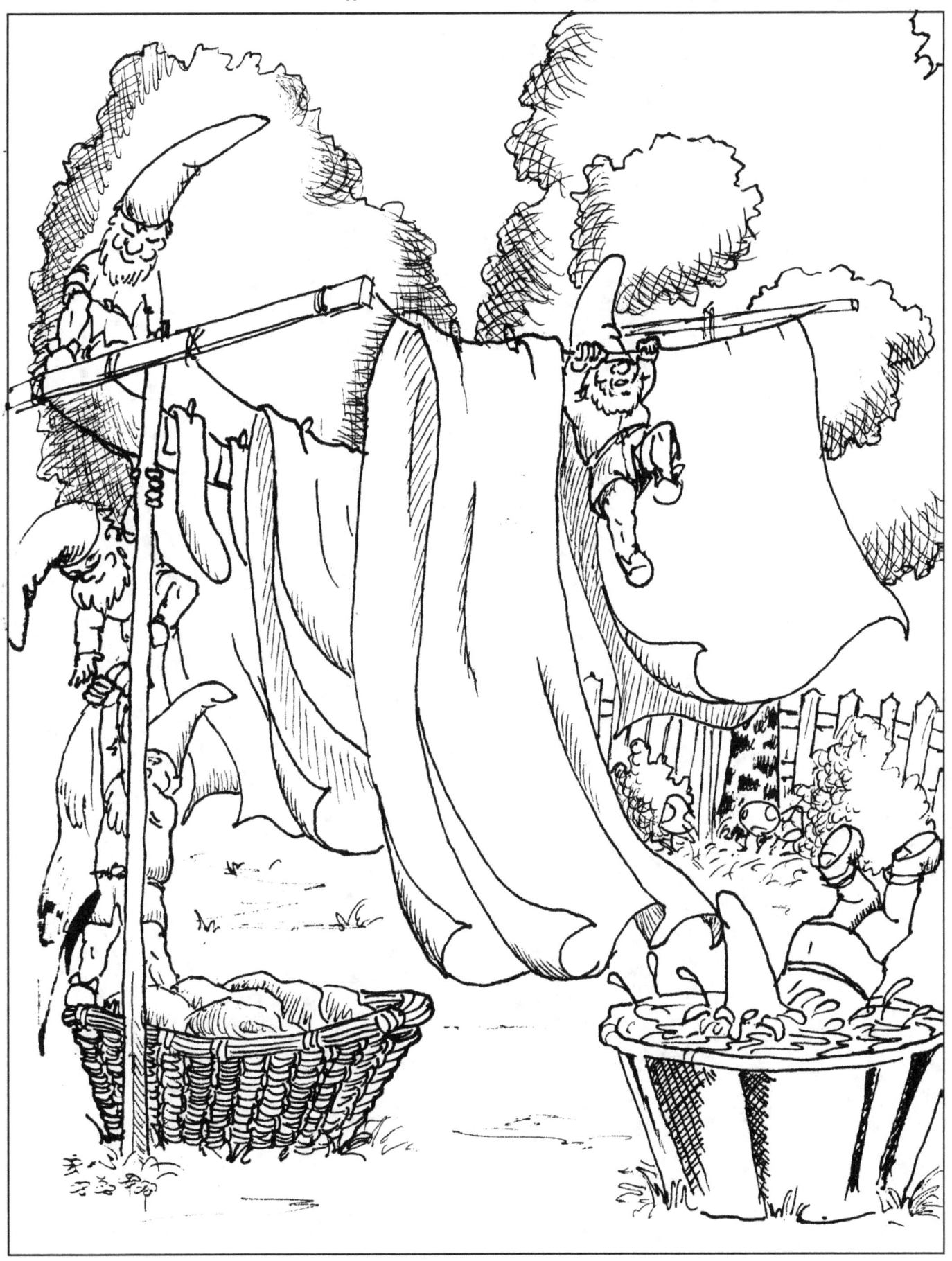

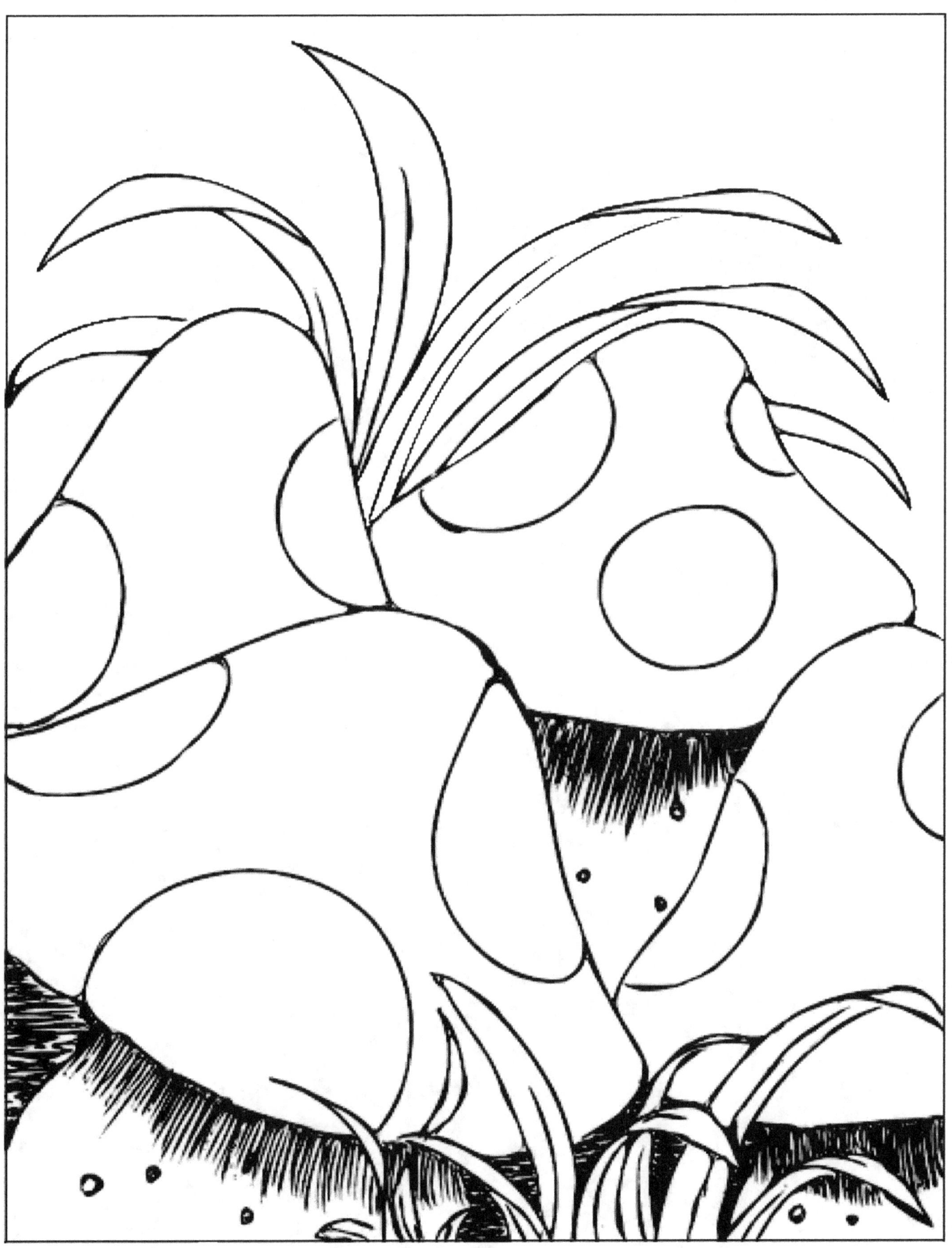

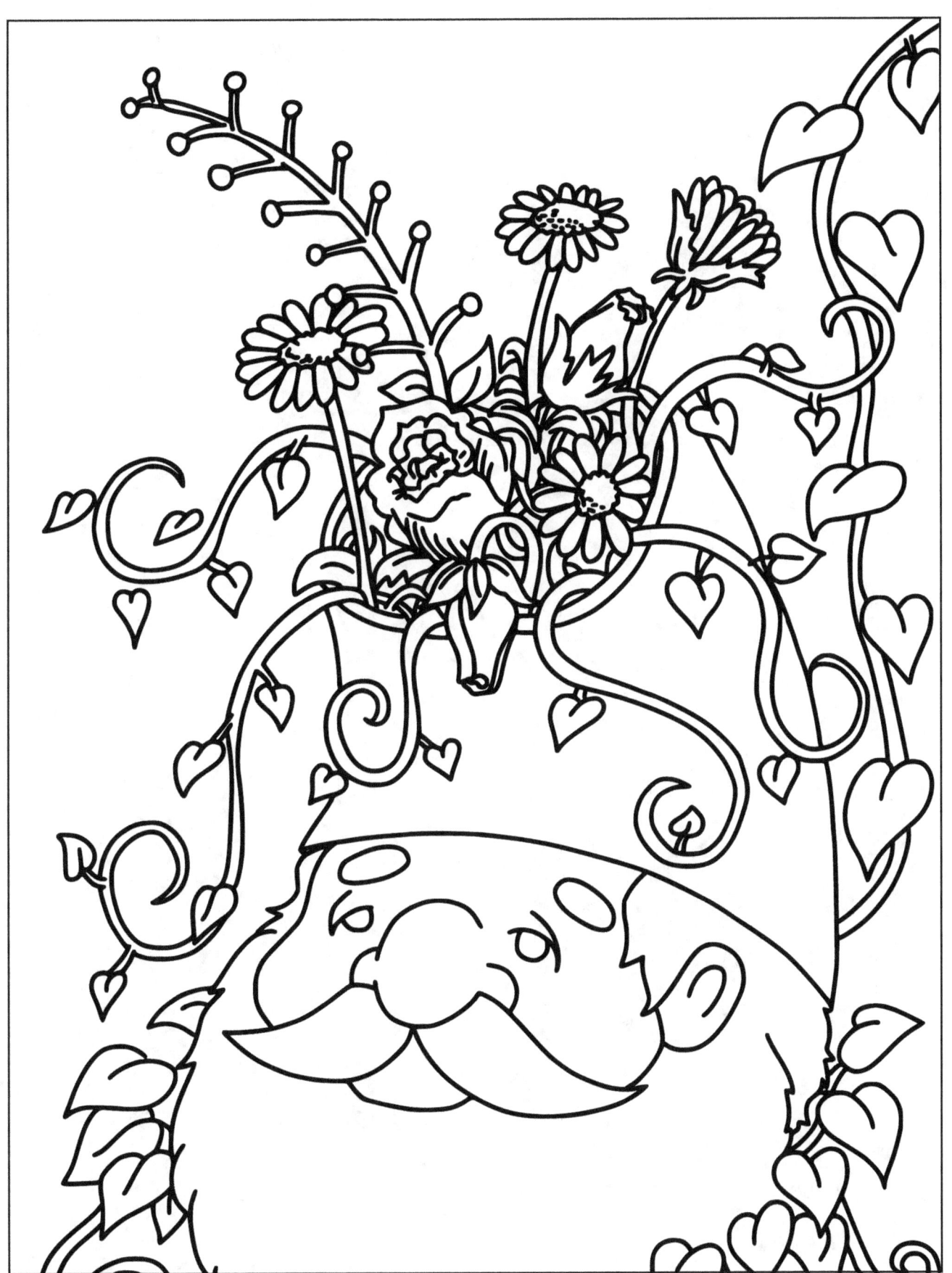

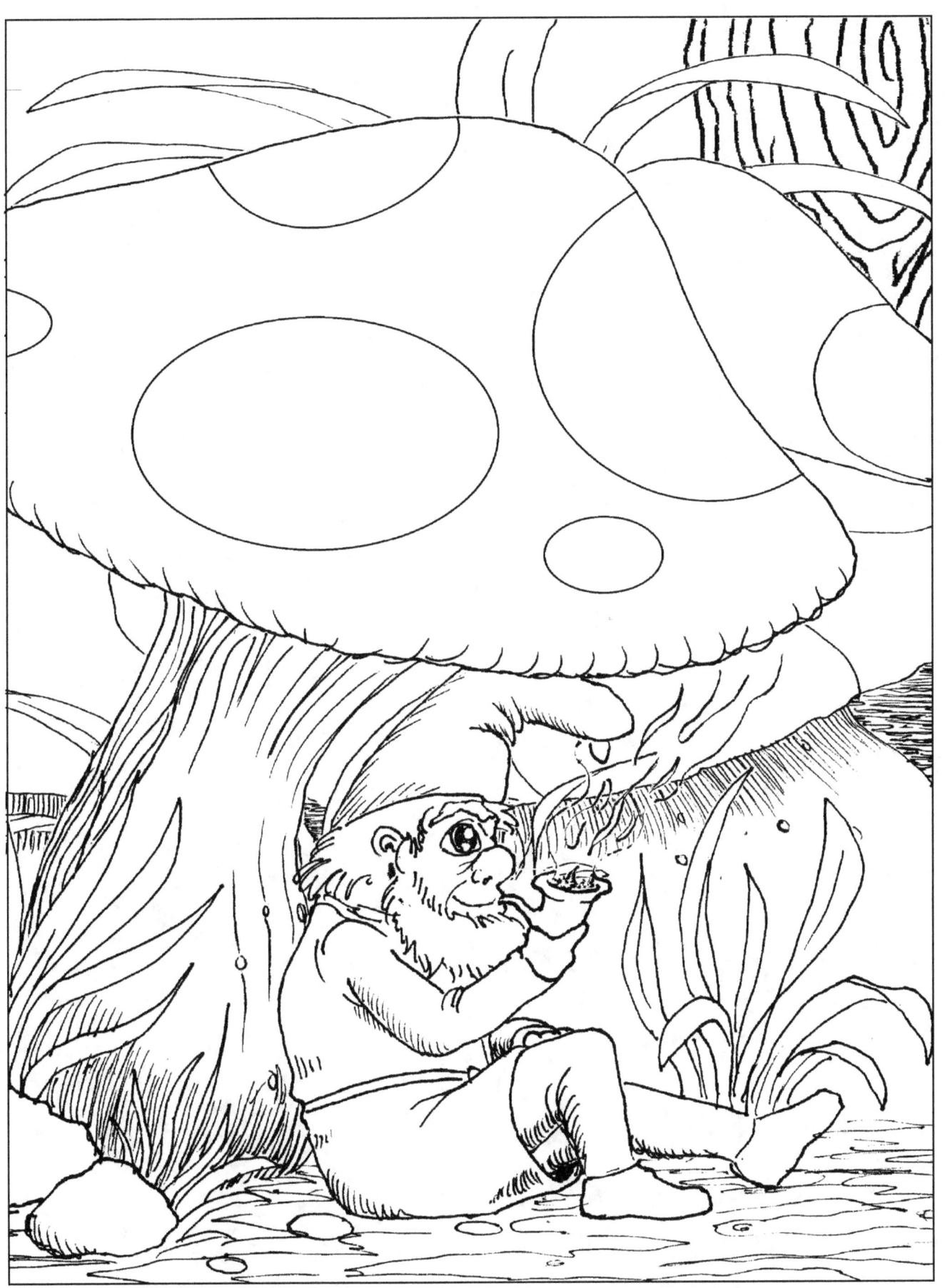

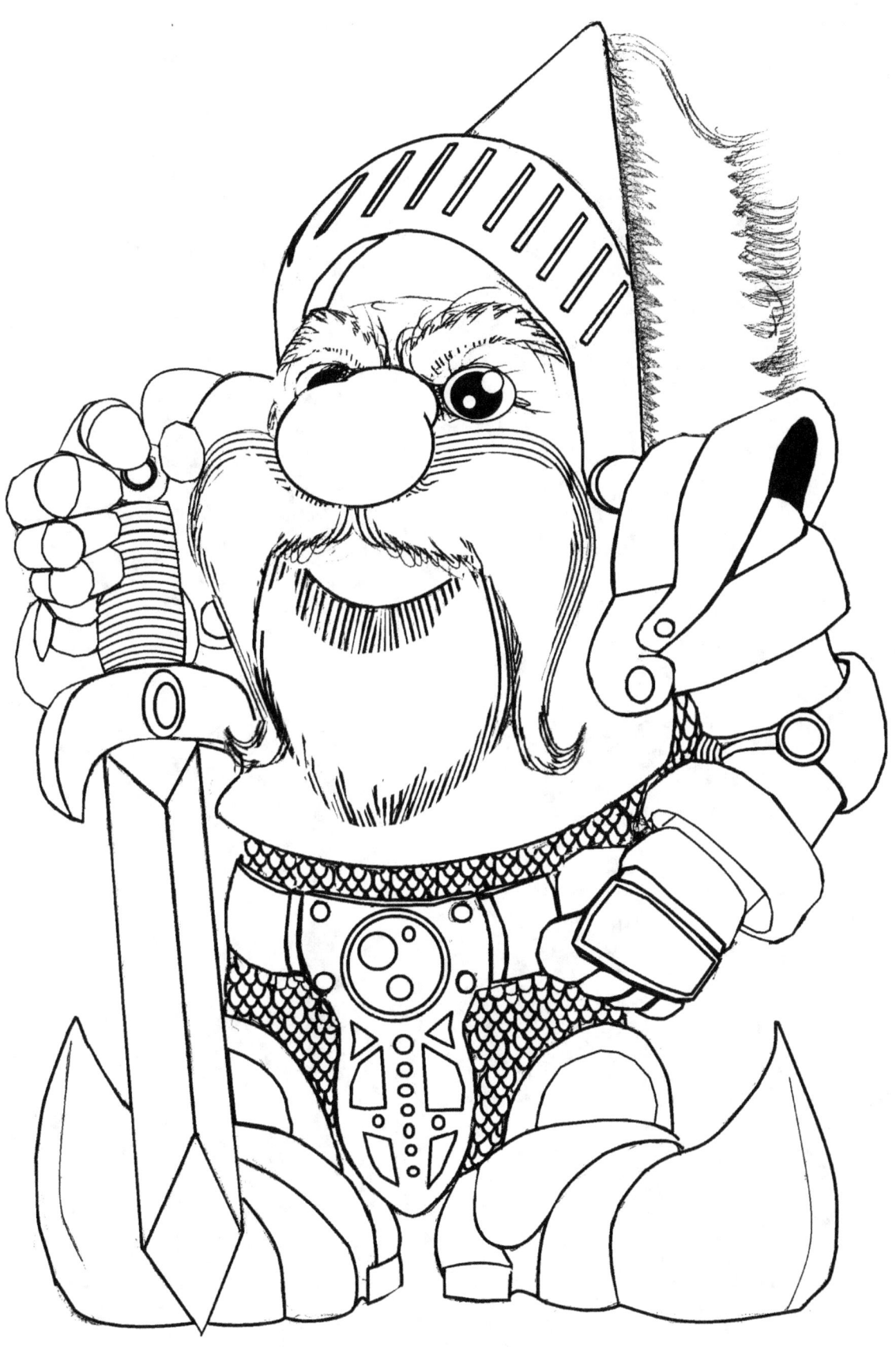

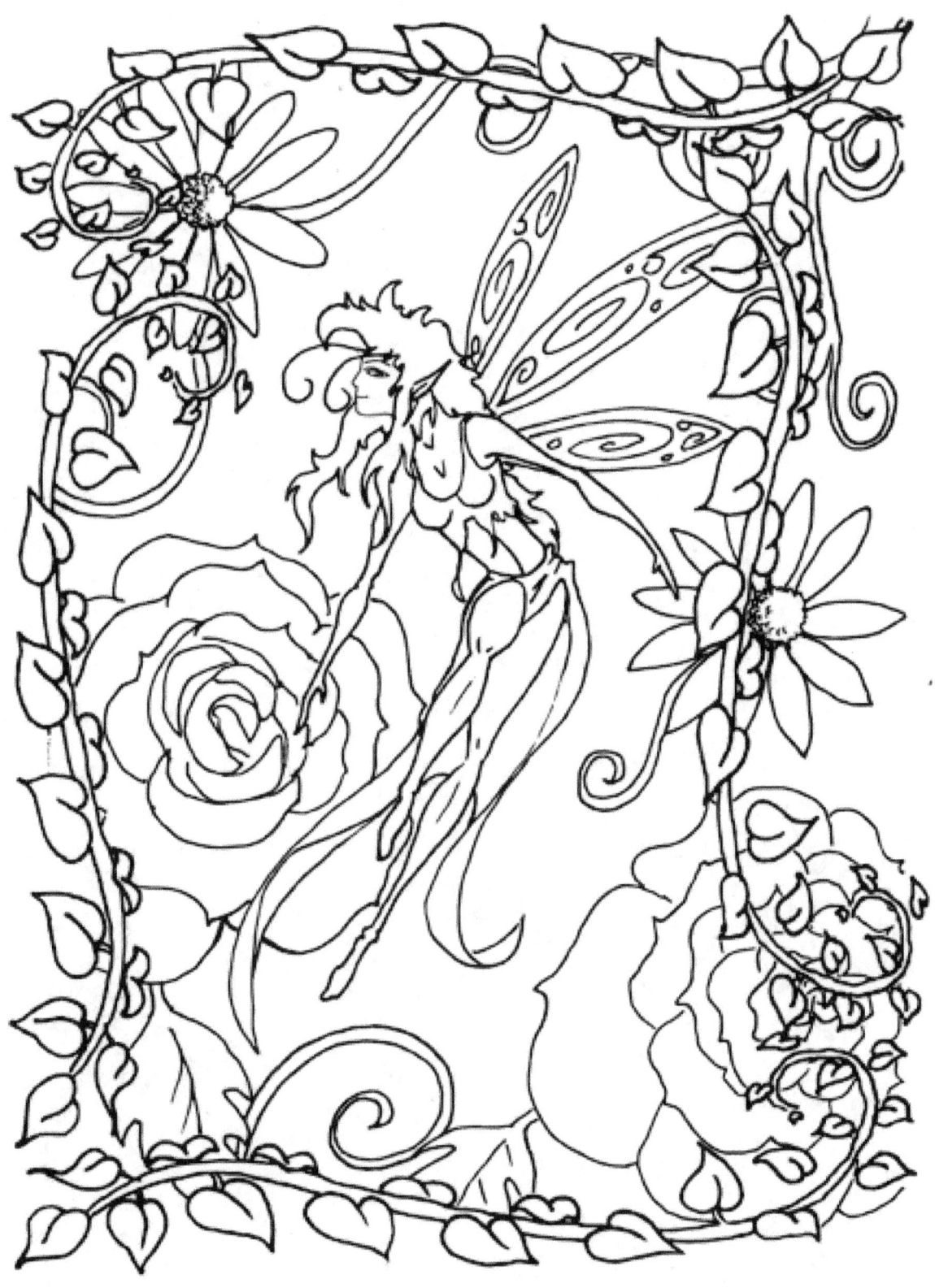

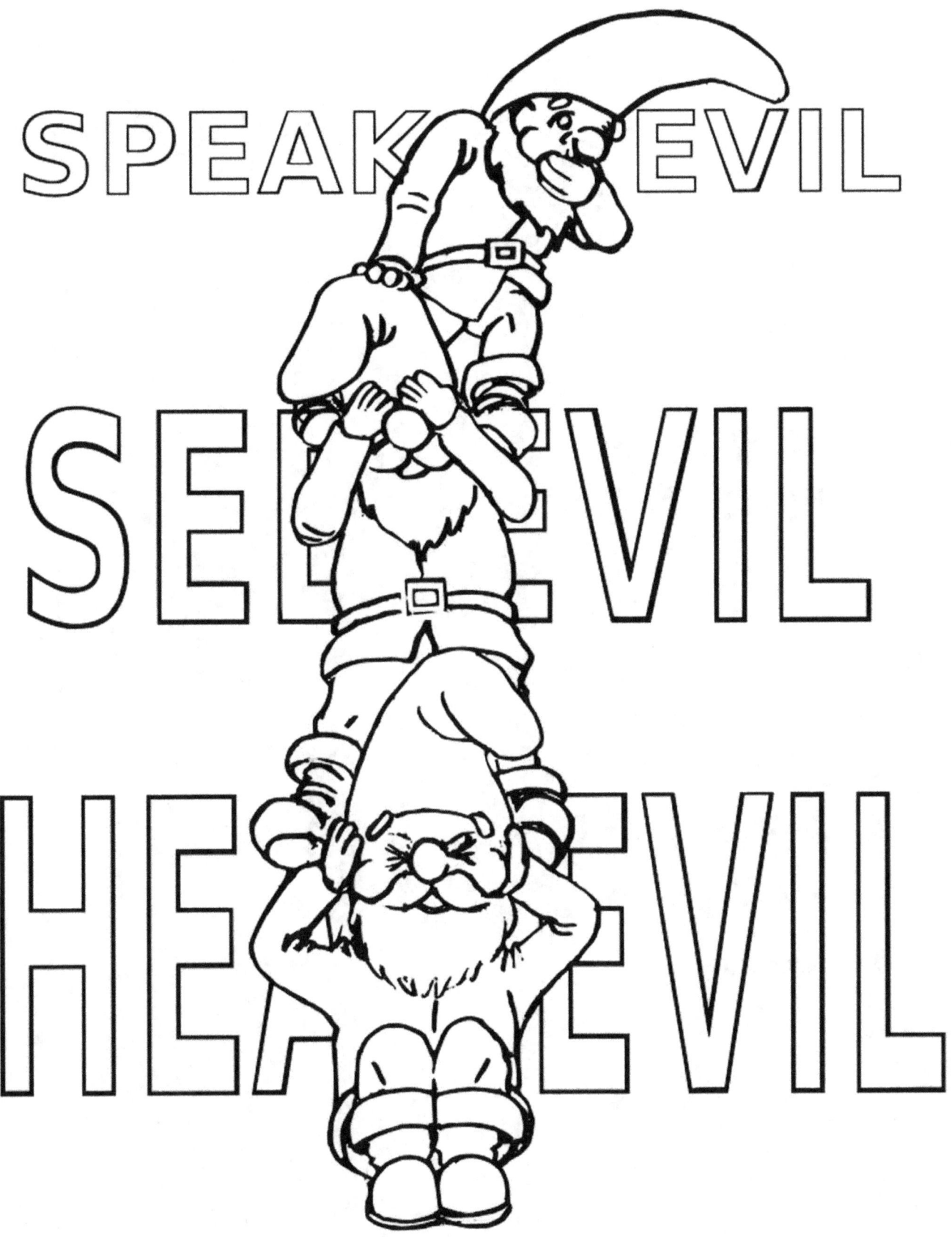

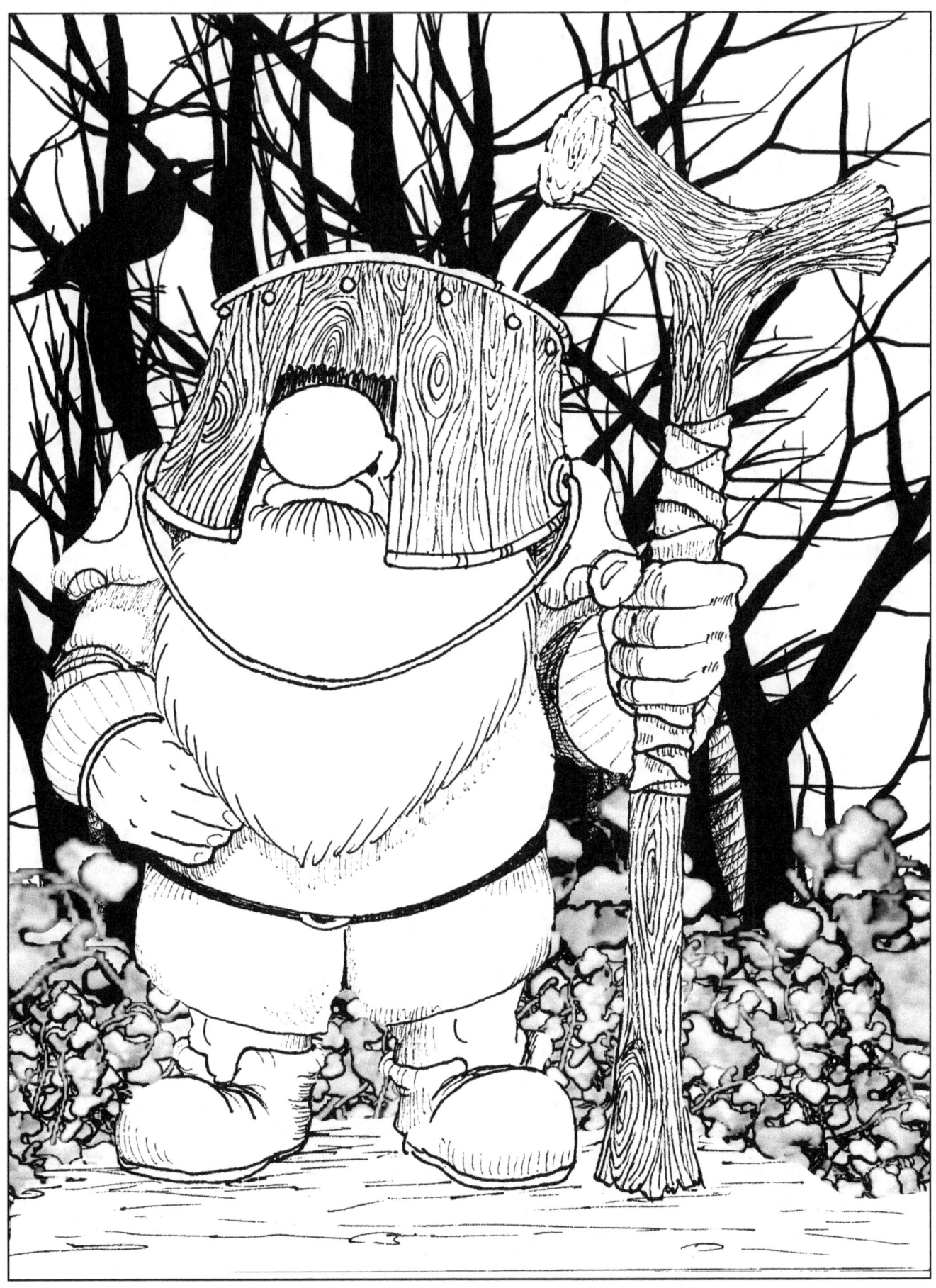

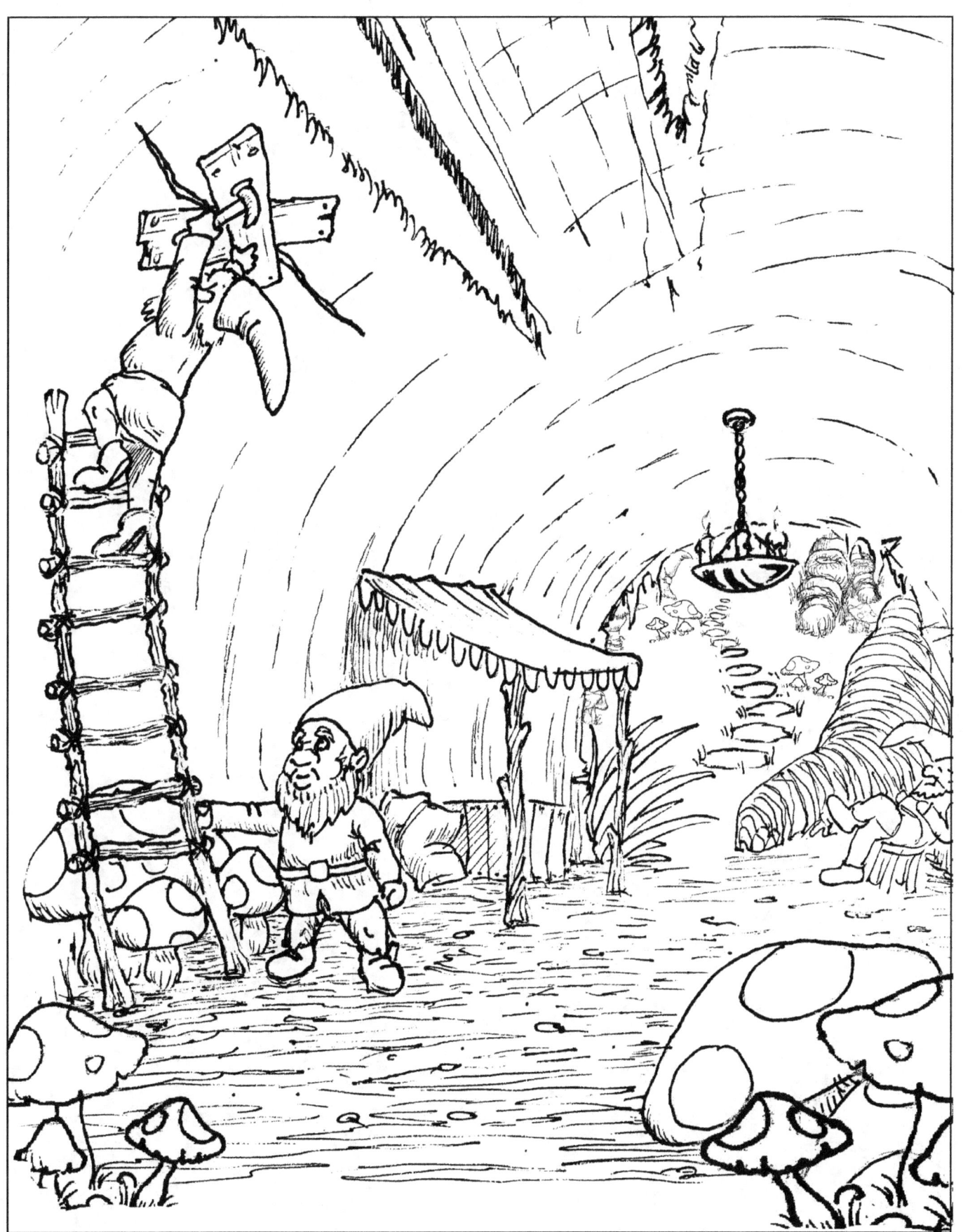

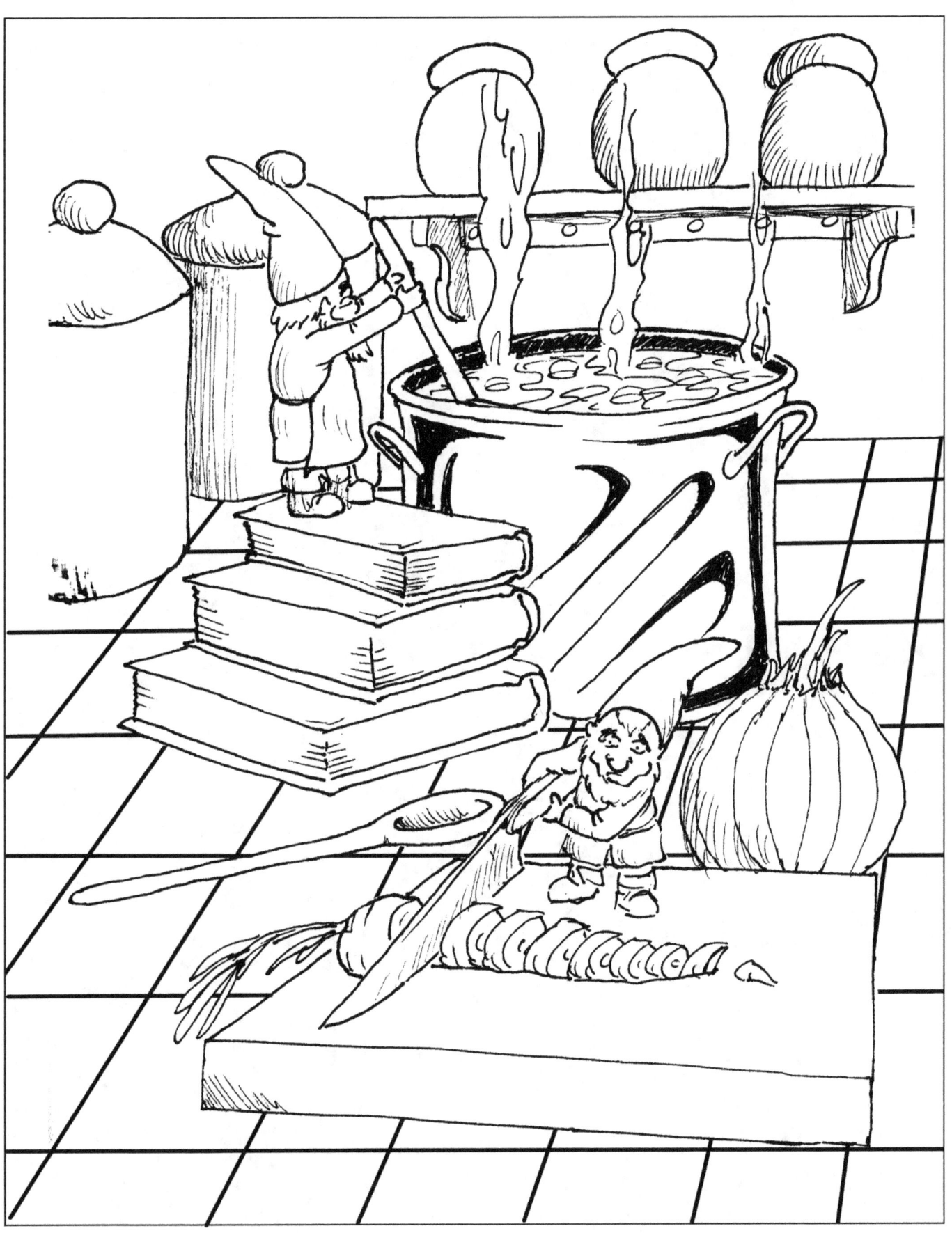

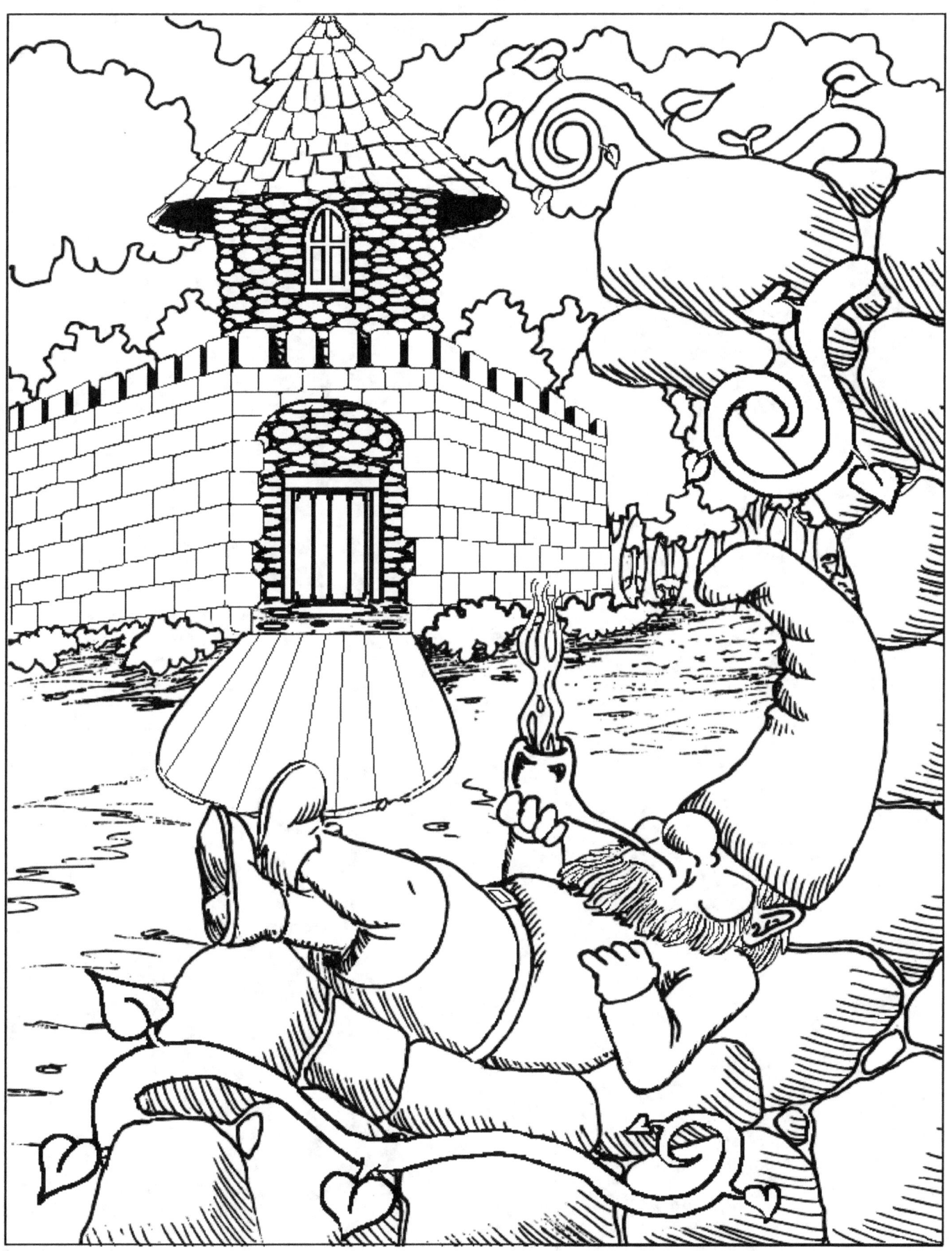

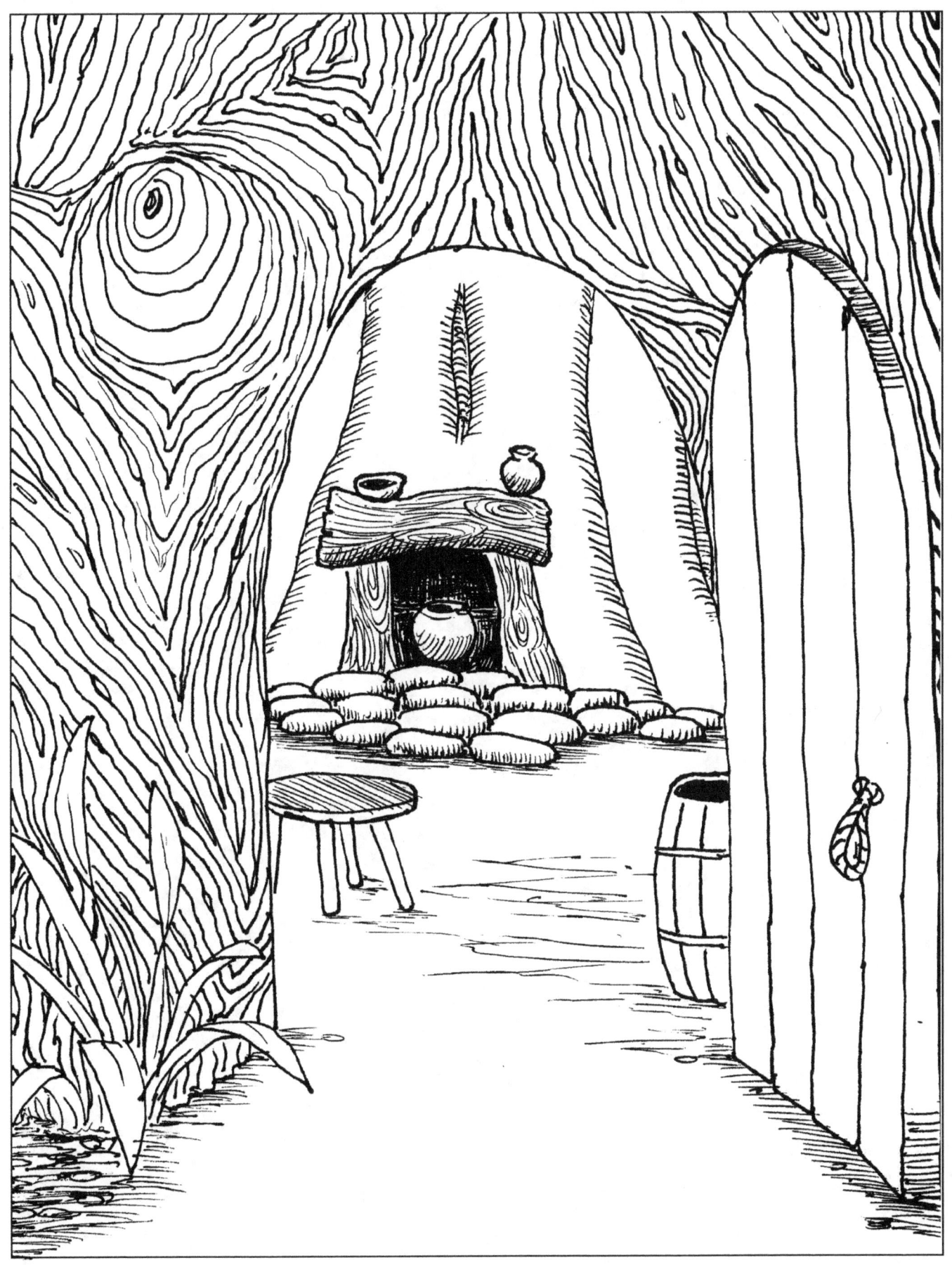

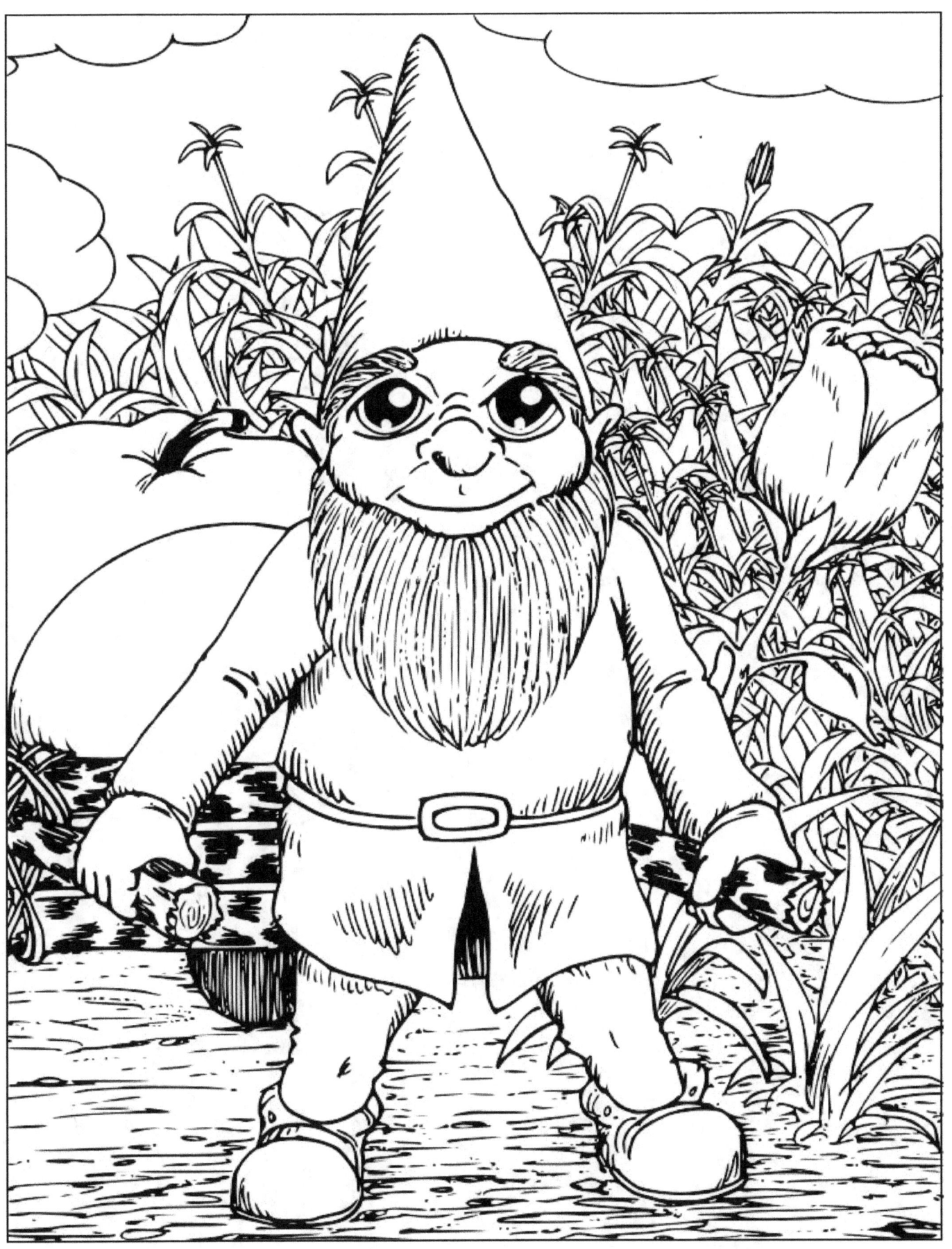

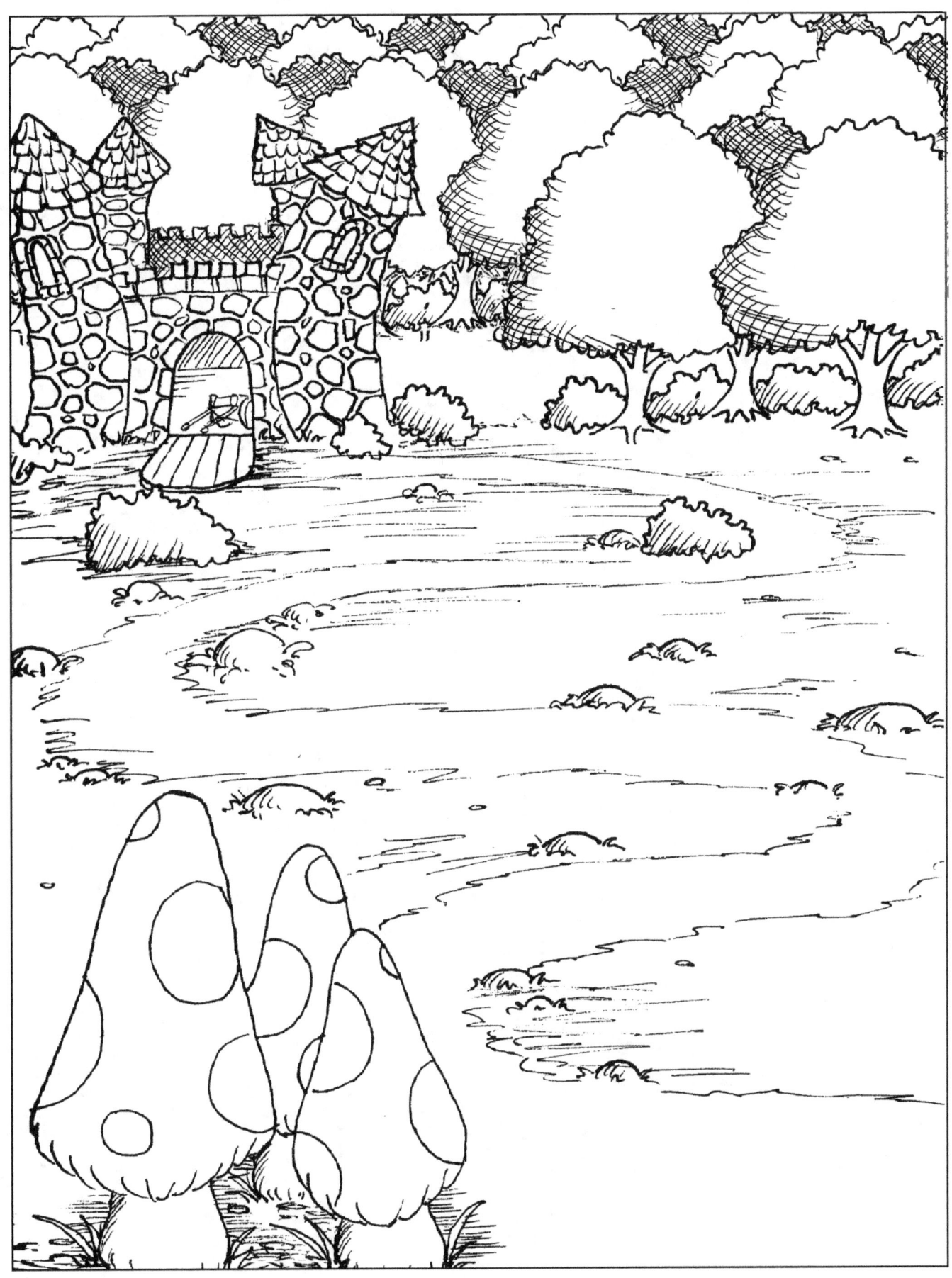

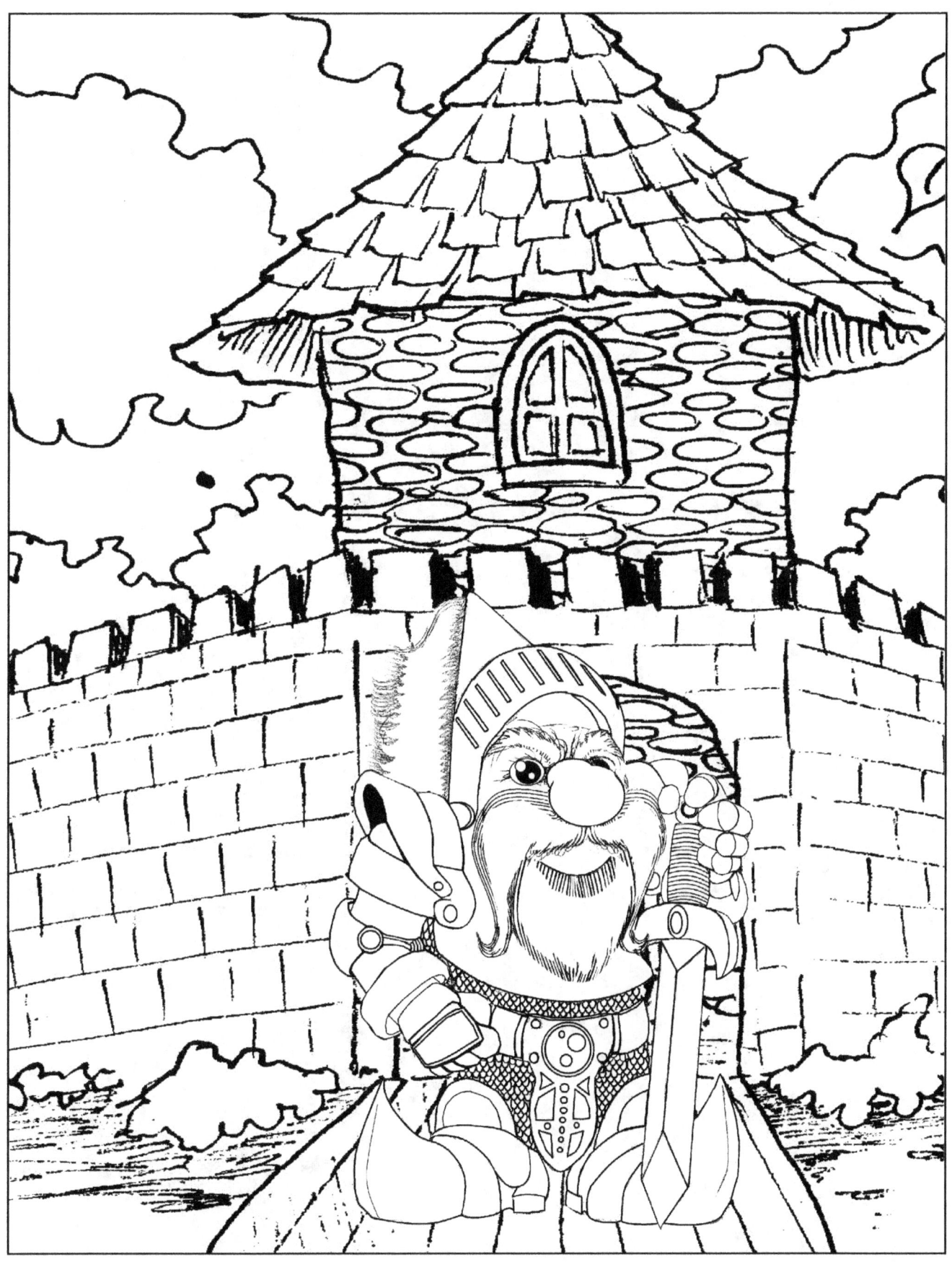

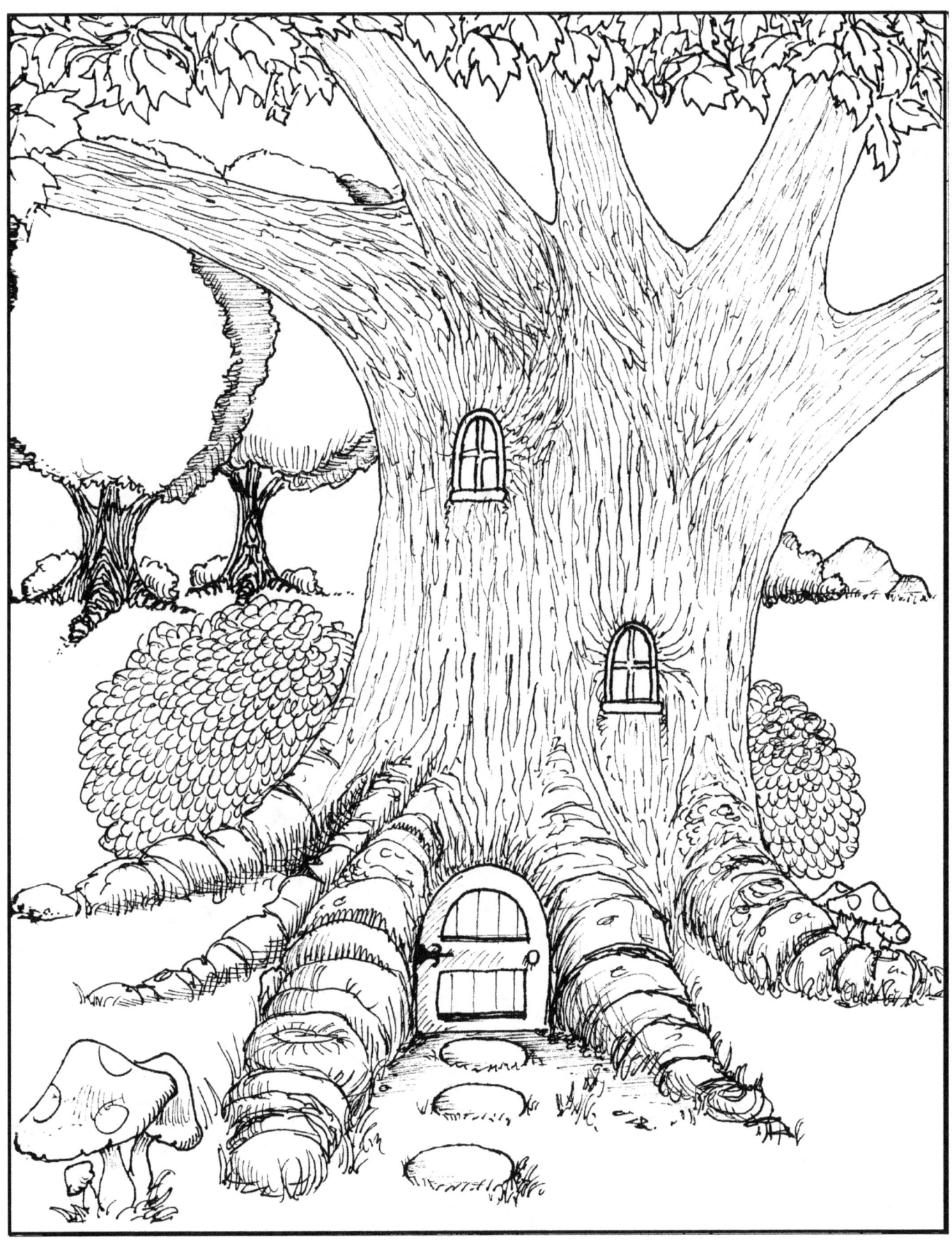

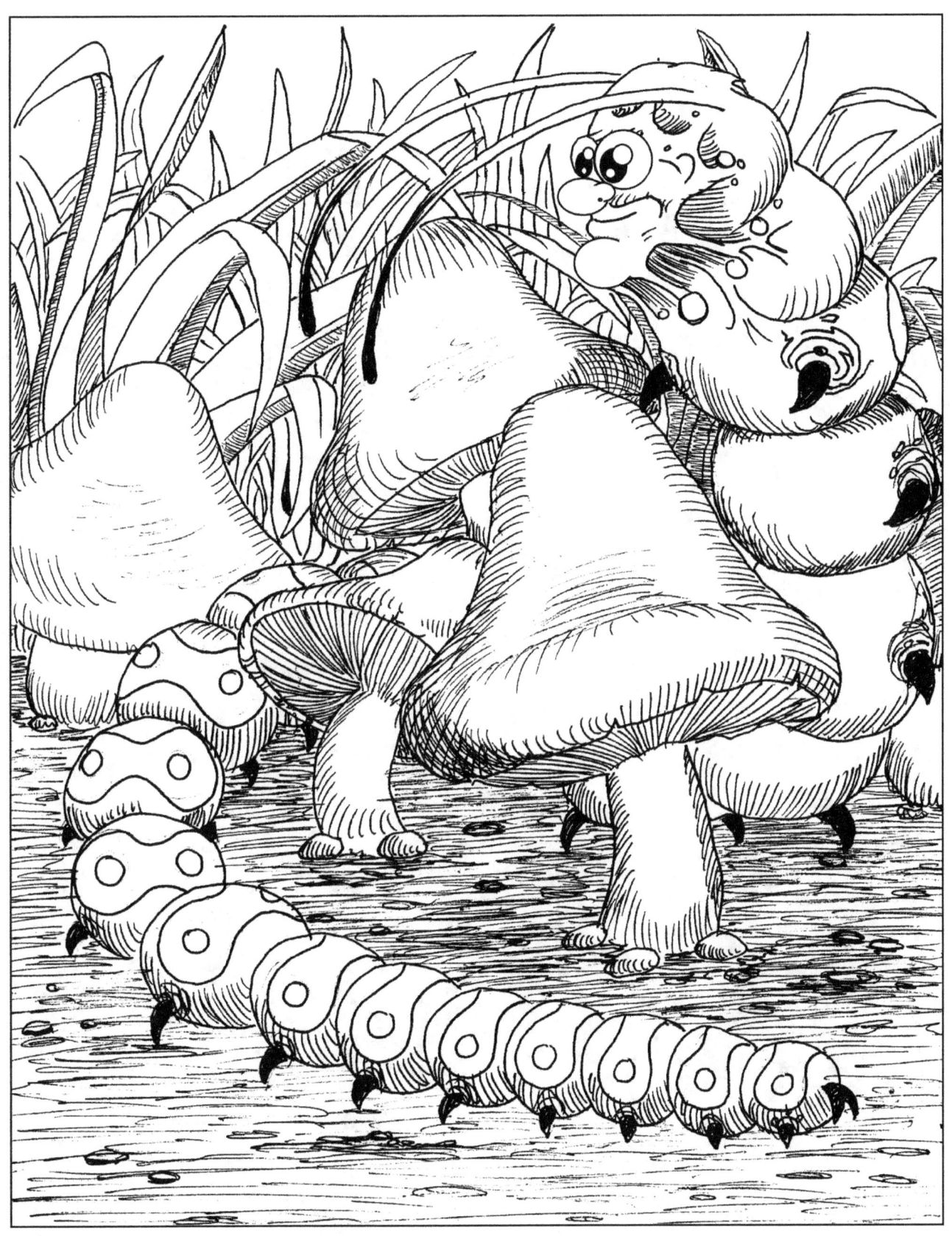

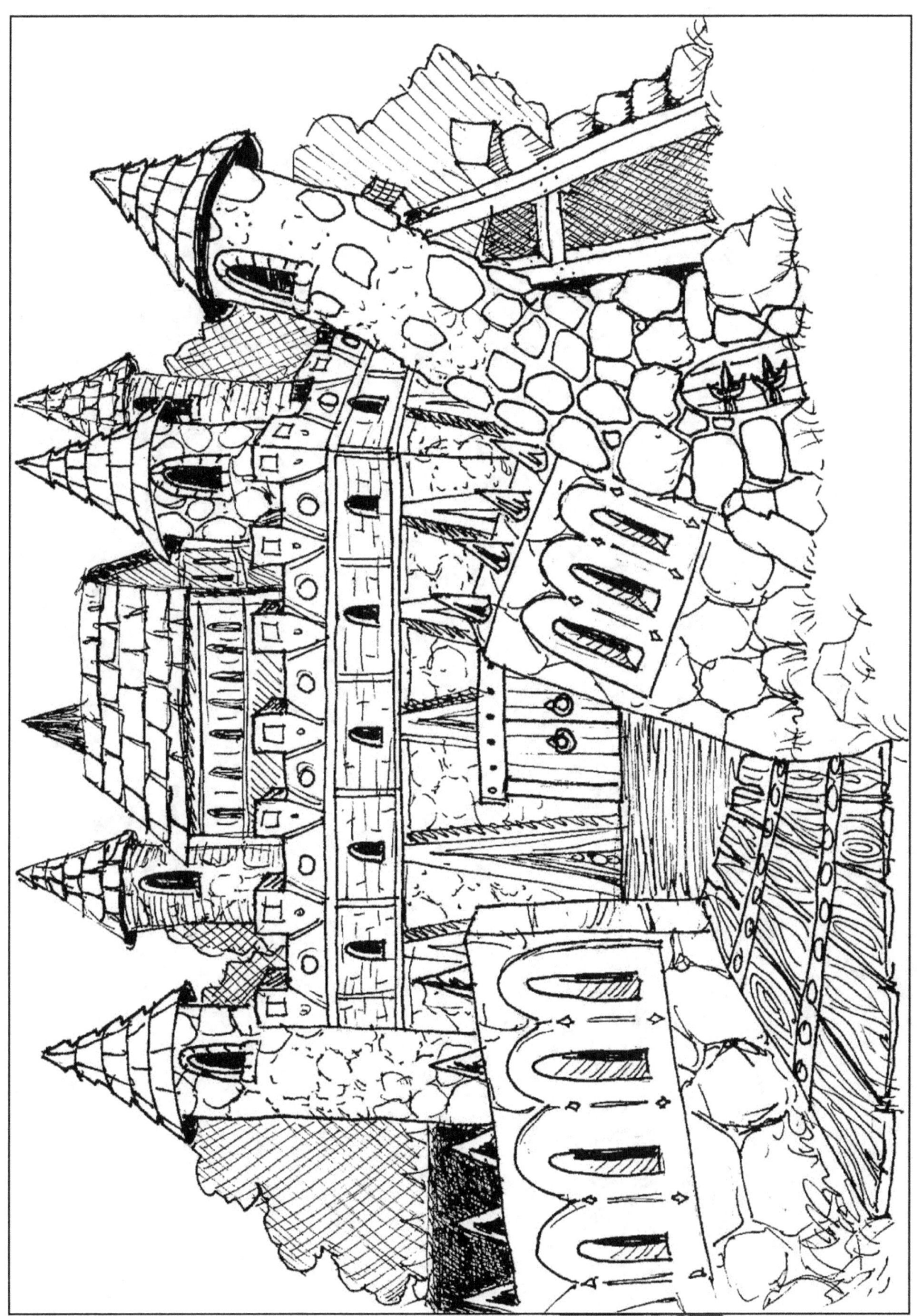

ABOUT THE ARTIST

Gnomes, an Adult Coloring Book of Gnomes Throughout Time, was created by Daniel Savage, an artist/illustrator from a very small Midwestern town where he lives with his wife and two children. He has been creating art in various forms since he was old enough to hold a pencil, and has worked in a wide variety of media from pen and paper to concrete and metal. His best creation has been his son who creates music and his daughter who has a budding art career of her own under the proud, watchful eye of her father.

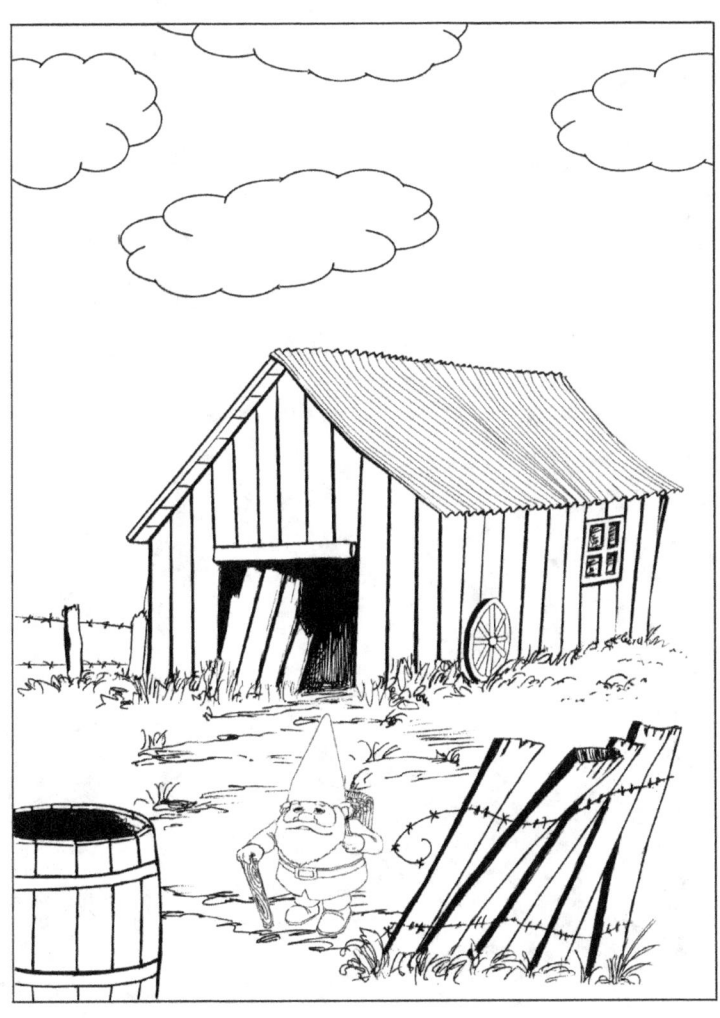

Use this page to test color combinations and as a blotter page

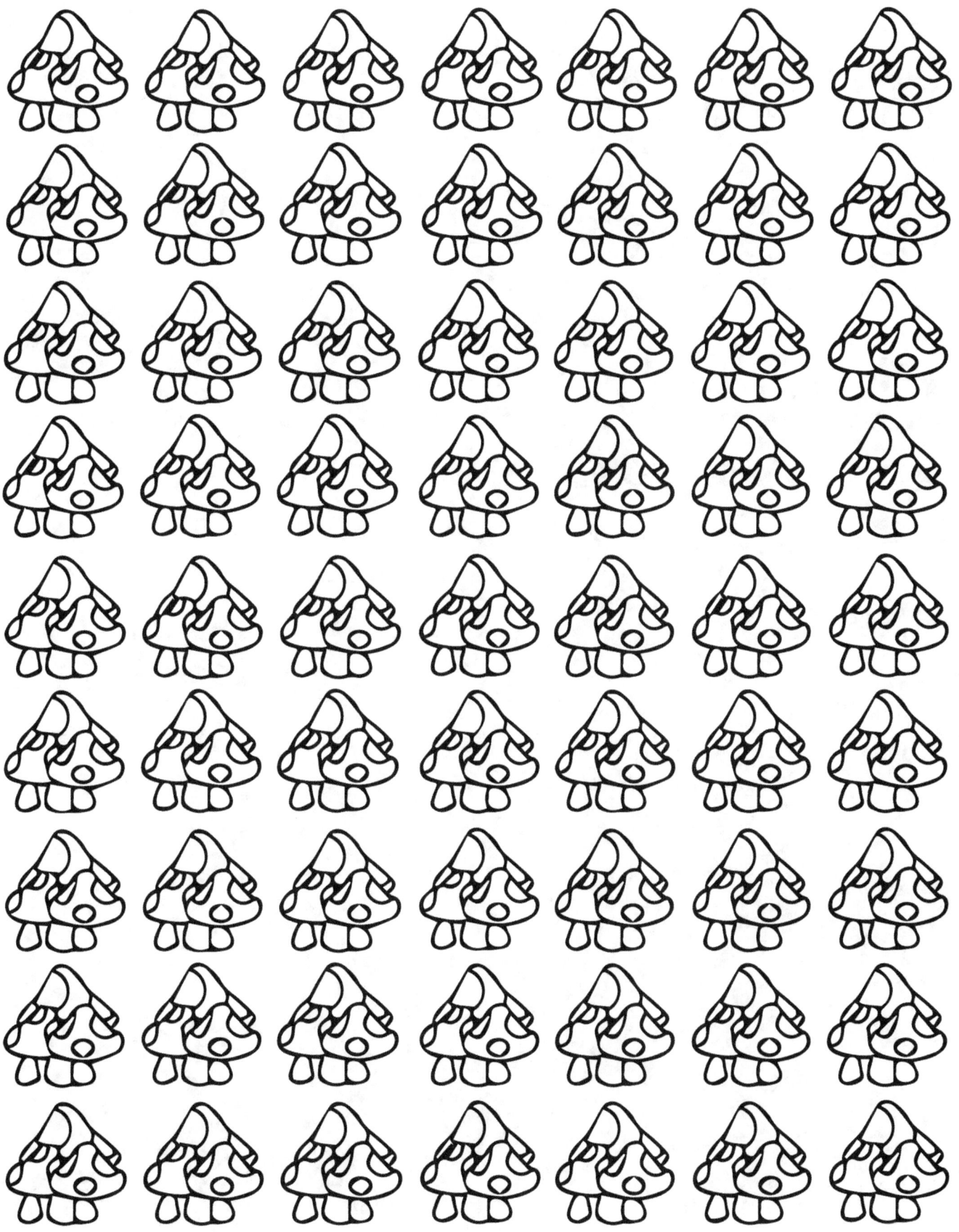

Use this page to test color combinations and as a blotter page

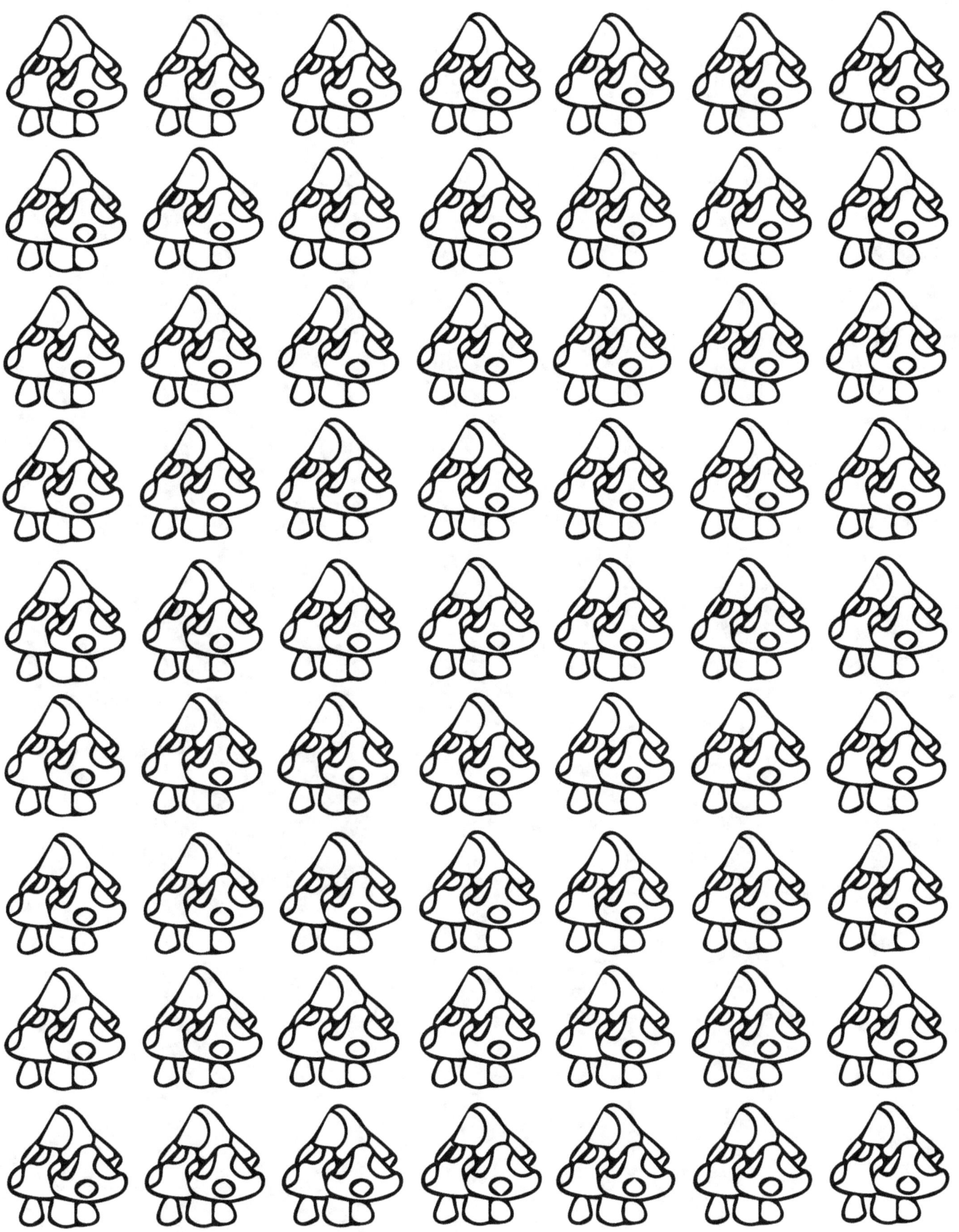

www.ingramcontent.com/pod-product-compliance
Lightning Source LLC
Chambersburg PA
CBHW060012210526
45170CB00017B/2340